HOW TO
INVEST
YOUR
MONEY
WITH A CLEAR
CONSCIENCE

THE CANADIAN GUIDE TO
PROFITABLE ETHICAL INVESTING

HOW TO INVEST YOUR MONEY WITH A CLEAR CONSCIENCE

Eugene Ellmen

James Lorimer & Company, Publishers
Toronto, 1987

Cover Design: Don Fernley

Canadian Cataloguing in Publication Data

Ellmen, Eugene.
How to Invest Your Money With a Clear Conscience
1. Investments — Moral and ethical aspects. 2. Finance, Personal — Moral and ethical aspects. 3. Investments — Canada. 4. Finance, Personal — Canada. I. Title.
HG4521.E55 1987   332.6'78'0971   C87-094467-3

James Lorimer & Company, Publishers
Egerton Ryerson Memorial Building
35 Britain Street
Toronto, Ontario M5A 1R7

Printed and bound in Canada
5 4 3 2 1 87 88 89 90 91

CONTENTS

ACKNOWLEDGEMENTS

Many thanks to all the people connected with the ethical investment movement who helped to give shape and direction to this project. Special acknowledgements go out to Larry Trunkey, who has done so much to nurture the Canadian Network for Ethical Investment. Thanks also to Mike Lewis of Westcoast Research and Information Cooperative, and to Larry Gordon of the Credit Union Central of Ontario.

I want also to thank my fellow *Money Monitor* writers at Canadian Press, Rob Macleod, Gord McIntosh and Brenda Dalglish. Their style has left its mark on this book.

To Naomi, for her love and patience, and for first suggesting that I write about socially responsible finance.

PREFACE

In the summer of 1987, life was pretty good for millions of Canadians. With the 1981-82 recession only a distant memory, many were plunging into a buying binge of houses, cars and furniture as well as indulging finer tastes in expensive wines and gourmet restaurants.

True, in September 1987 the unemployment rate was still a depressing 8.6 per cent. But this was down from 8.8 per cent in August and 9.5 per cent a year earlier. Housing construction was booming, corporate after-tax profits were up and retail sales in August totalled $12.8 billion, 8 per cent higher than in August 1986. For many consumers, this buying binge was financed through salary-draining mortgages and credit-card balances carried for months at a time. Still, employed Canadians generally felt content, even if they did owe a lot of money to the bank.

This mood of optimism was reflected on Canada's stock exchanges. Celebrating the fifth anniversary of a bull market of rising stock prices, more than three million Canadians held stock directly or through increasingly popular mutual funds. Commentators in the financial press were warning that shares were dangerously overbid, selling for more than 20 times their annual earnings. Nevertheless, stock exchange indices continued to inch their way up. By mid-August, the 300 index of the Toronto Stock Exchange reached its highest point ever.

When the bubble burst, it burst with a bang. On Black Monday — Oct. 19 — investors fled the market with a vengeance and the TSE 300 fell by 11 per cent, erasing $37 billion from stock values. By the end of the week, the 300 index was 14 per cent lower. At the time of writing, the market was still declining and it was not clear where, or when, stock prices would bottom out.

Black Monday signalled more than just an adjustment in share prices — it forecasted a change in which Canadians will spend and invest their money. Clearly, the freewheeling era of the mid-1980s is coming to an end as Canadians look for financial havens and investments promising real value. A week after the debacle, hundreds of Canadians lined up at banks and other financial institutions to buy that most secure of Canadian investments — the Canada Savings Bond.

Given such uncertainty about the financial future, you may well ask whether it is safe to invest your money according to your conscience. It may be fine to worry about matching your investments with your values during good times, but should financial security become the overriding concern when the economy gets shaky? Has "ethical" investing become an unaffordable luxury?

The answer to this question depends on your specific holdings, but, generally speaking, the risk of investing in ethical enterprises is not necessarily higher than the risk posed by conventional investments. Because well-managed, socially responsible companies can avoid consumer lawsuits and environmental clean-up orders, they stand to earn conservative, but steady, returns. Likewise, a guaranteed investment helping to finance a co-op housing project has at least the same level of deposit protection as an account with the Bank of Montreal.

Furthermore, the financial panic that gripped world stock exchanges following Black Monday may well present some opportunities for ethical investors. Ethical mutual funds that were overpriced in the summer of 1987 may now be more affordable. Stocks in most companies meeting various ethical standards became cheaper, although it was unclear whether they had hit bottom.

Still, this does not address the issue of the need for ethical investment. While the ethical investment movement became popular during a time of relative prosperity, the test of its mettle will come during the unsetled economic times ahead.

If inflation and interest rates are going to rise during the next few years, as many forecasters predict, the people who will suffer the most will be those on the margins of our economy, such as young workers settling into their first jobs, employees of aging industrial plants and pensioners on fixed incomes. Faltering economic growth will lead to an increase in unemployment, and may also quicken the pace of deregulation — an obsession of conservative-minded governments in the 1980s. A variety of social programs could be axed in this mood of deficit-cutting conservatism.

So if there ever is a period in which ethically directed investment is needed, it is during a period of uncertain economic prospects. Progressive, people-oriented goals become harder to achieve during rocky times as business interests press for deficit reduction and cuts to social safety nets. Ethical investors, by directing capital to socially useful enterprises, can do their own small part in stabalizing the economy and in ensuring that our country's social priorities continue to be met.

Eugene Ellmen, October 1987

INTRODUCTION

Each trade agreement, each new bank loan, each new investment is another brick in the wall of our continued existence.
— John Vorster, Prime Minister of South Africa from 1966 to 1978

Ideas have hands and feet. They work for you.
— Dr. J.J. Tompkins, one of the founders of the Antigonish, N.S., cooperative movement

For many people the term "ethical investment" is a contradiction in terms — like jumbo shrimp or military intelligence. They wonder how it is possible to participate in the dog-eat-dog world of finance and still maintain their values.

These people — and perhaps you are one of them — handle their financial affairs in a mechanical way. They choose a bank because it is close, they park RRSP money in a trust company and forget about it, and, when it comes time to buy an investment, they let a stock broker make their decision.

Yet, making financial decisions need not be divorced from ethical and social considerations. Even if you only write cheques, make payments on a car loan or mortgage, or use a credit card, there are ethical alternatives to pursue. If you are one of more than three million Canadians with an RRSP, there are ethical places to hold those RRSP savings. If you pay taxes, as more than fifteen million Canadians do, there are ethical tax-savings strategies to investigate. If you are retired, and you want to find a secure place for your retirement savings, many financial institutions provide ethical investment opportunities. Finally, if you are one of the growing number of Canadians investing money in stocks, bonds or mutual funds, there are a host of ethical possibilities for you to explore.

WHAT IS ETHICAL INVESTMENT?

How does ethical investment differ from conventional investment? First, a definition. Ethical investment can be defined in two ways: 1) the screening out of particular investments that fail to meet certain specified ethical criteria; and 2) a positive choice of investments that fulfill certain social objectives. The second type of investment is sometimes referred to as "alternative investment" to distinguish it from socially screened investment.

In conventional or traditional investment, no attention is paid to the ethical purposes or social consequences of money. It is invested solely according to financial objectives. Conventional investors ask whether their money is secure, whether the investment will generate interest income or stock dividends, whether their capital will grow in value, and whether the investment requires time and know-how to manage. If political or social factors are taken into account at all, they are considered simply for the risk they pose to the financial performance of the investment.

THE QUESTION OF PROFIT

The issue of profit, or rate of return (in investment language), is a nagging question for professional advisers connected with the ethical investment movement. One of the most common questions they are asked by prospective investors is "Do I have to sacrifice return to invest my money according to my values?"

This question will be dealt with in greater detail in each chapter of this book, but generally speaking investors should expect a reasonable rate of return on their ethical investments, except in cases where they consciously sacrifice earnings to accomplish certain ethical objectives.

For example, the "Roses" savings account at Bread and Roses Credit Union in Toronto, a community credit union sensitive to social investments, offers zero interest. It also offers other accounts at slightly below market rates, but the "Roses" account appeals to some people who are willing to sacrifice a return to accomplish social objectives.

Investors in the Ethical Growth Fund, one of several Canadian ethical mutual funds, earned about 9 per cent on their money in the year up to June 30, 1987. While this was a respectable return, it was lower than the average of Canadian equity funds, which posted a one-year gain of 17.7 per cent, according to *The Financial Post*.

One of the companies favoured by some ethical investors, Jannock Ltd., has profited shareholders handsomely. A lucky ethical investor could have purchased stock in the company, which holds interests in brick, steel, high-technology and sugar companies, for as low as $4.30 a share in 1982, and made many times his or her money by selling in 1986 for as high as $30.75.

BALANCING ETHICAL AND FINANCIAL CONSIDERATIONS

No two ethical investors have the same portfolios (collection of stocks or other investments) because no two ethical investors have the same ethical and financial objectives. For example, many ethical investors avoid shares in Varity Corp., formerly Massey-Ferguson Ltd., because of its 20-per-cent interest in Fedmech Holdings Ltd., a South African farm-equipment company. Others stay away from companies such as Devtek Corp., a leader in Canada's growing military industry. The particular investments that get screened out vary according to the ethical priorities of the individual.

Ethical investors interested in placing money with socially creative and positive investments may choose institutions such as community-development credit unions, which invest money in non-profit organizations, cooperative enterprises and small business. Or they may support one of a growing number of community-loan funds, which help finance projects by local entrepreneurs or community businesses.

However, as an ethical investor you not only have to decide what ethical priorities are most important, you have to establish a set of financial objectives. Because of this, you must balance your financial objectives with your ethical considerations. This is not always an easy process, and sometimes you may have to accept a lower financial return or a higher level of risk if you want to meet certain ethical objectives. Conversely, sometimes you may refrain from purchasing an ethically acceptable investment because it is too costly or otherwise unfavourable from a financial point of view.

For example, consider the situation of a woman investor who — for financial reasons — has decided to put $5,000 in a mutual fund. These funds pool stocks or other investments and manage them on behalf of the investors. If this woman adheres to a feminist philosophy that opposes pornography, she will want to avoid investments in the pornography industry. Accordingly, she may choose Investors Summa Fund, a Canadian fund that refrains from buying shares in companies involved in pornography. Summa also screens on other issues.

So far, so good. But she has heard that there are other mutual funds, such as the Ethical Growth Fund, which also screen for social criteria. Ethical Growth seeks out companies that encourage good employee relations and operate in countries promoting racial equality. It also focuses on non-military and non-nuclear companies. She may appreciate these concerns, but for her as a feminist, pornography is a big consideration. So, for ethical reasons, she still favours Summa.

Before she actually signs over her cheque, she again returns to financial considerations. She checks the financial performance of the funds and the acquisition fees charged by the funds. In the case of Summa, there is an 8.5-per-cent acquisition fee. For Ethical Growth, the fee is 5 per cent. (For some other funds, there is no fee at all.) This means that $425 will be taken right off the top with a $5,000 investment in Summa, and $250 will be taken with Ethical Growth. Her concern with pornography will cost her at least $175 as soon as she signs over the cheque.

Of course, she stands to regain that $425, and more, when the fund earns dividends and capital gains. But that money taken from the top and handed over to fund managers and sales representatives is money that could be earning a return for her in the future.

This book will deal with these and other kinds of ethical and financial issues, presenting the various social criteria of different investments, as well as the financial considerations that investors and other consumers of financial services should always keep in mind.

THE GROWTH OF THE ETHICAL INVESTMENT MOVEMENT

The ethical investment movement dates to the 1970s, when church, environmental and peace activists began purchasing shares in companies to enable them to sponsor resolutions at annual meetings. Corporate executives came to dread the uncomfortable, pressing questions posed by these activists at meetings that had traditionally been attended by quiet, complacent shareholders. At one famous meeting in 1984, a Greenpeace activist attempted to give Inco Ltd. chairman Charles Baird a dead trout to press home Inco's responsibility to reduce its acid rain emissions. Company officials would not let him in the room.

This shareholder activism spurred individuals to ask their stockbrokers or other investment advisers to recommend investments that do not pollute, or that do not have South African investments. Recognizing a need, several U.S. church groups and stock brokers established mutual funds to pool stocks or other investments according to socially responsible criteria. Based on their success, several Canadian organizations followed suit.

The movement was given a boost — and a name — in 1983, when the Canadian Conference of Catholic Bishops released *Ethical Rejections on the Economic Crisis*, a stinging condemnation of the failure of capitalism to respond to the ethical obligations imposed by the lingering recession of the early 1980s.

The report was dismissed by many business leaders as wooly-minded, or downright subversive, or both. But it captured the imagination of scores of different kinds of Canadians — both religious and non-religious — who were working in a number of ways to make the economy responsive to human needs. Peace and church activists, environmentalists, unionists, community workers, consumer advocates and progressive investors all welcomed its people-centred stance. They also adopted the report's language, particularly its concern with the place of "ethics" in economics.

As a result, ethical economic behaviour came to include more than just good and honest conduct. The new view was that business has an obligation not only to raise the profits of shareholders but to be a good corporate citizen. This means that corporations should act to preserve the environment, treat their employees fairly, refrain from actions that exploit people in other nations and behave in a variety of ways that fulfill their obligations to the wider society.

With the emergence of this new sense of corporate responsibility, ethical investment organizations soon appeared. Larry Trunkey, a Victoria investment adviser faced with a growing list of clients asking for ethical investments, founded the Canadian Network for Ethical Investment, a group of investors, investment professionals and interested individuals. The organization published its first newsletter in the fall of 1986. In 1987 a Toronto company, Ethicscan Canada, was formed to provide investors with information on the ethical performance of selected companies.

Investors of all ages are demanding these services and products, but investment professionals say that so-called Baby Boomers are the most vocal. Born between the late 1940s and early 1960s, this generation is now between the ages of twenty-five and forty-two, a time in life when jobs, careers, families and finances become a concern. However, ethical investment advocates are adamant that many Baby Boomers want more than just investment opportunities — they want to express their social values through their investments. Says Trunkey:

> Some of the members of Pollution Probe in their high school days are now junior executives and they are driving BMWs and they make good salaries. But if you talk to these people, you will find that they are not that far apart on values. A lot of these people are trying to come to grips with their values and integrate their lives. As more of the Baby

Boomers become investors, they are starting to reflect upon
their money as a proxy for themselves.

Despite the movement's recent history, a split of sorts has emerged in
it. While ethically oriented stockbrokers and large investors believe
that investment should be used to improve the ethical performance of
corporations, others in the movement believe that investments should
be directed toward community organizations that will provide
economic power and jobs to disadvantaged people in distressed communities. The question seems to revolve around whether it is better to
reform capitalism through ethical investment, or establish new
enterprises through alternative investment. As the Reverend Tim Ryan
of the Scarborough Foreign Mission Society said in the July 1985
Report on Business magazine: "A corporate economy run by a strong
élite unaccountable to any constituency would be wrong even if they
were making ethical decisions."

THINKING ABOUT ETHICAL INVESTMENT

In Canada, the ethical investment movement has spawned many initial products, but few prescribed programs; a number of investment
suggestions, but no overarching strategies; a variety of possibilities,
but no all-encompassing packages. In short, people entering the ethical investment movement can try out a number of different approaches
to managing their money but there are few places where they can park
their money and forget about it.

The spirit of the ethical investment movement does not centre on
the sale of particular products or services that are "politically correct."
It centres on a particular way of thinking about your finances — the
conviction that it is possible and desirable to invest your money in a
way consonant with your values.

The aim of the ethical investment movement is to encourage financial consumers to think clearly and thoroughly about their financial
decisions and ethical priorities. It would not be much of an advance —
in financial affairs or in social well-being — if people simply replaced
the mechanical decision-making of traditional personal finance with
an equally mindless, but "politically correct," approach to personal
finance.

If ethical investors embrace this more general aim, they stand to
gain control over their financial lives, and learn something about themselves along the way.

1

SAVING AND BORROWING — THERE'S MORE THAN JUST THE BANKS

The oil rigs of Alberta and the cattlefields of Brazil may seem half a world away from your neighbourhood bank, but economic troubles in those far-away places are changing the way banks handle your everyday money. Canada's Big Five chartered banks are discovering that the international and energy loans that promised big profits in the 1970s are turning into the albatrosses of the 1980s.

Faced with these problems, the banks have renewed a romance with their most important customer — the Canadian consumer — in an effort to shore up sagging profits on corporate and international loans. While the banks traditionally have been followers rather than leaders in the introduction of new consumer financial services, they are now embracing the retail marketplace, providing consumers with a dizzying array of new banking services. The new services include everything from full-service chequing accounts to personal lines of credit.

This unprecedented marketing war for your deposit dollar is creating confusion for many consumers, but it is also heightening awareness of the services offered by financial institutions. Consumers are becoming more aware of their banking needs, more willing to spend time shopping for financial services and more concerned about purchasing financial services tailored to their circumstances. "The customer must be shown clearly that he or she is getting a better deal," said Peter Rose, a U.S. finance professor, in the May 1987 issue of *Canadian Banker*. "And that better deal must be accompanied by greater convenience and lower transaction and search costs."

The new consumer consciousness is having an impact on more than just the choice of accounts. Canadians are shopping around for institutions that they can feel comfortable with from a social point of view — as well as ones that give a good deal on their money. "Regardless of whether you disapprove of service charges or whether you disapprove of anti-social behaviour, like investing in South Africa, it doesn't matter," says James Savary, a York University economics professor and banking critic for the Consumers' Association of Canada. "There are alternatives out there."

For consumers interested in matching their social values with their everyday banking needs, credit unions provide a progressive alternative to the banks. They are owned by customers — not stock market investors — and they have a solid record of investing in local communities. Credit unions also have a good record on relations with their employees and many are helping to finance innovative community projects to develop local economies.

Before looking at the banking services you need, and how credit unions stack up against banks and trust companies on those services, we should look at how credit unions differ from the other deposit-taking financial institutions.

CREDIT UNIONS — A DEMOCRATIC AND LOCAL ALTERNATIVE

The banking industry in Canada is dominated by the big chartered banks and a handful of conglomerates that control large trust companies. The largest of these giants is the Royal Bank of Canada, the biggest financial institution of any kind in the country. The astounding size of banks like the Royal can be appreciated only by looking at their annual reports. In 1986, the Royal owned nearly $100 billion in assets and made almost $500 million in profit. In terms of assets, the Royal is three times larger than Canada's biggest industrial enterprise, Ontario Hydro. Even with its huge nuclear- and water-generated power plants, electrical transmission systems and transformer stations, Hydro reported only $31.4 billion in assets in 1986.

The chartered banks wield enormous economic power in Canada. Figures contained in *A Framework for Financial Regulation*, a 1987 report for the Economic Council of Canada, show that the four largest institutions controlled 52 per cent of the assets of all banks, trust and loan companies and insurance companies in 1984. Only seventeen institutions were needed to account for 80 per cent of the assets.

By comparison, Canada's cooperative financial institutions are large in number, but small in size. An estimated 4.2 million English-speaking Canadians are members of about fifteen hundred credit unions. Likewise, more than four million francophones are members

Table 1

Canada's 10 Largest Financial Institutions, 1987

	Assets ($mil)	Net Income ($mil)	Employ- ees	Major Share Holders
Royal Bank of Canada	99,607	488.9	38,186	Widely-held
Bank of Montreal	87,180	352.95	32,988	Widely-held
Canadian Imperial Bank of Commerce	80,841	341.2	33,914	Widely-held
Bank of Nova Scotia	64,013	336.2	26,215	Widely-held
Toronto Dominion Bank	51,447	402.6	20,211	Widely-held
National Bank of Canada	27,872	186.85	11,274	Widely-held
La confédération des caisses populaires Desjardins du Québec[1]	25,646	181.8	22,344	Member federations
Caisse de dépôt et placement du Québec[2]	25,072	1,892.6	193	Quebec gov't 100%
Canada Trustco Mortgage Co.	24,095	133.9	10,247	Imasco 99%
Trilon Financial Corp.	21,751	128.0	20,724	Brascan 38% Olympia and York 11%

Source: The Financial Post 500, Summer 1987.
[1]The Desjardins group is a confederation of *caisses populaires* in Quebec. It includes assets of local *caisses populaires,* member-federations and Caisse centrale Desjardins.
[2]The Quebec government pension fund.

of about fourteen hundred *caisses populaires.* In Quebec, this loyalty to credit unions is so strong that there are more branches of *caisses populaires* than there are of banks. La Confédération des caisses populaires Desjardins du Québec, an umbrella organization for *caisses populaires*, is so large that it is estimated to be the the seventh-biggest financial institution in the country.

The character of the credit-union movement has roots in the social and economic climate of Quebec at the turn of the century. The first credit union in the country was founded in 1900 in Lévis, Quebec, by Alphonse Desjardins, a journalist who had turned to publishing the debates of the Quebec legislature and the House of Commons. Struck by observations in the course of his work that usurious moneylenders were gouging the poor with interest rates as high as 100 per cent, Desjardins turned to the growing People's Bank movement in Germany for a popular solution to put the lenders out of business.

Desjardins set up a bank — called a *caisse populaire* — to allow any person to purchase a share, deposit savings and loan money at reasonable rates to other members. The important difference between Desjardins' bank and conventional banks was that the *caisse populaire* asked for no collateral to back a loan. Instead, the *caisse* loaned money based on members' assessment of the character of the borrower. The *caisse* was a risky business for Desjardins, who personally held liability for bad loans. It was not until 1906, when Quebec passed the first credit-union legislation in North America, that directors of *caisses populaires* no longer held personal liability.

Desjardins' movement grew rapidly in Quebec and the burgeoning *caisses populaires* proved to be both a social and a financial success. In the first thirty-five years of their existence, *caisses populaires* loaned $200 million and suffered a loan loss rate of only .05 per cent. To this day, personal lending continues to be the cornerstone of credit-union activity, a type of borrowing that is relatively safe for lenders because, unlike corporate borrowers who have limited liability, individual borrowers are personally responsible for their loans.

English Canada followed Quebec's lead. In the 1920s Dr. Moses Coady, a passionate reformer, helped to establish scores of credit unions in the Maritimes through the Antigonish Movement of St. Francis Xavier University. At the same time, the ravages of the Depression encouraged prairie farmers to form credit unions after the banks choked off farm credit. In the decades that followed, credit unions proliferated throughout English Canada. Today, local credit unions hold more than $45 billion in assets, a figure that is even higher when provincial and national credit union organizations are taken into account.

For many communities, a credit union or *caisse populaire* provides the only local banking facility. The Economic Council of Canada study already cited notes that of the 672 localities in Quebec that are served by only one financial institution, 95 per cent are served by a cooperative. In Saskatchewan, there are 201 communities with only one financial institution, 68 per cent of which are served by a credit union.

DEMOCRATIC OWNERSHIP

How do credit unions and *caisses populaires* differ from banks and trust companies? Perhaps the most important distinction concerns ownership. In order to become a customer of a credit union, you must become a member. As a member you are given one vote along with all other members. One of the operating guides for credit unions puts it this way: "In a credit union, the members are the owners of the business. Only the members can use its services and receive direct benefit from its operations. It is a cooperative enterprise that has democracy or democratic control — the rule of the people — as one of its most important principles of operation."

Credit unions are organized around "bonds of association." This means that members of a credit union must have some common characteristic that links them into a community. In community credit unions, members are all residents of the same city or area. In other cases, credit unions may be composed of people in a profession, employees of a company or members of an ethnic group.

By contrast, Canadian banks and trust companies are owned by their shareholders. In the case of the banks, the ownership is dispersed among tens of thousands of individual shareholders. With such a widespread ownership, bank management holds firm control over the policy issues affecting the banks. In the case of trust companies, ownership is often held by a small coterie of individual businessmen through huge conglomerates. Canada Trust, for example, the country's largest trust company, was taken over in 1985 by Imasco Ltd., a British-controlled tobacco and food conglomerate. Royal Trust, the country's second-largest trust firm, is part of Trilon Financial Corp., controlled by the Brascan Ltd. empire of Edward and Peter Bronfman, a branch of the Bronfman family that made it big in the Seagram liquor business. Another big chunk of Trilon is held by Olympia and York Developments Ltd., owned by the wealthy Reichmann family of Toronto.

In order to have a say in the policy of a bank or trust company, you must buy stock in that institution. Then, the voice that that stock delivers must be heard against the voices of thousands of other shareholders or, in the case of a trust company, against the voices of wealthy individuals who have voting control of the company sewn up.

In a credit union, you have one vote as a depositor or creditor. As a member, you have the right to vote for the board of directors, help set policy at annual meetings and sit on policy committees. All credit-union members have the option to become intimately involved in their credit union, even if only a minority actually choose to do so.

Some banking groups, particularly the American Bankers Association, argue that credit union members have allowed their institutions to drift away from the ideals of the credit-union movement in order to attract more customers, offer more services and compete with the banks. "Many credit unions have expanded far beyond the compact, personal, self-help groups of the past, and have become large, impersonal institutions interested primarily in growth," states an ABA booklet on credit unions.

Gary Gillam, legal affairs director for the Credit Union Central of Ontario (the Ontario umbrella organization) concedes that there are som credit-unio director wh "sometime thin tha th member exist for the well-being of the credit union, instead of the reverse." Generally, however, he says the social foundation of the credit-union movement is strong: "People who go out and serve on credit-union boards are giving up Tuesday evenings in June when they could be watching a ball game. People who do that have an interest in their community and their members' well-being that gives credit unions a very different feeling from other financial institutions."

David Levi, former chairman of the Vancouver City Savings Credit Union — the largest credit union in Canada and second-largest in the world — admits that VanCity cannot do the kind of personal lending carried out by credit unions serving fishing villages along the B.C. coast. But he makes no apologies for VanCity's size: "VanCity is really a community credit union and our community is greater Vancouver. We're a reflection of the people who live in greater Vancouver. We're a full-service operation, which means we offer everything that other financial institutions offer, plus a lot more."

THE SOCIAL RECORD

As an ethically minded consumer of financial services, you want assurance that the money you place in a credit union, bank or trust company winds up in socially useful investments. At the same time, you want to know whether or not the institution you help to support through your business is a good corporate citizen. Does it have a good record on labour relations and support for community causes?

While there is no all-encompassing review of the ethical record of credit unions compared with other deposit-taking institutions, a look at several social criteria shows good reason to believe that ethical investors will be more comfortable placing their money in credit unions.

Investments

Banks, trust companies and credit unions earn a profit by loaning to businesses and individuals the money you deposit. The financial institutions charge a higher rate of interest to their borrowers than they return to you as a depositor. As an ethical investor, you essentially lose control of your money when you deposit it. Consequently, you will want some assurance that your deposit will not be used in ways that contravene your values.

Of all the social issues facing financial institutions, international lending has been one of the most troublesome. The issue has harmed the public image of the banks, which have a substantial proportion of assets invested abroad. Only a tiny number of credit unions have assets outside of their own communities, and trust companies do not do substantial business outside of North America. Critics of the banks have focused on two issues: loans to South Africa, and loans to the repressive régime of Chilean dictator Augusto Pinochet.

First, we should deal with South Africa. After much prodding in the 1970s by the Taskforce on the Churches and Corporate Responsibility (TCCR), which represents Canada's major churches, Canadian banks have agreed not to make any new loans to the South African government or its agencies. With regard to companies in South Africa, the banks are now reluctant to extend loans to such firms, but they have not made any official commitment to change this policy.

The Bank of Montreal appears to be the biggest Canadian lender to South Africa, followed by the Bank of Nova Scotia. The Bank of Nova Scotia will not disclose its private-sector loans to South Africa; but researchers for the California-Nevada Interfaith Committee on Corporate Responsibility have estimated that the Bank of Nova Scotia's total 1985 loans in South Africa may have amounted to as much as $50 million.

With regard to Chile, the Canadian banks helped to finance nearly $1.5 billion in loans in the five years following the 1973 military *coup* that overthrew the socialist government of president Salvador Allende. (This figure is supplied by the Latin American Working Group, a Toronto-based organization conducting research on links between Canada and Latin America.) The money was loaned directly by the banks, or in concert with other international banks. The Royal Bank led the pack with fifteen transactions, the Bank of Nova Scotia had six,

Table 2

Canadian Bank Loans Outstanding in South Africa

Bank	Loans to South African Gov't and its Agencies	Total Outstanding Loans (Gov't and Private Sector)
Bank of Nova Scotia	Under $10 million (1985)	Bank will not disclose
Bank of Montreal	Bank will not disclose	$54 million in 1984
Canadian Imperial Bank of Commerce	Bank will not disclose	Less than $5 million U.S. in July 1986
Royal Bank of Canada	Bank will not disclose	Under $8.7 million in 1985
Toronto Dominion Bank (1987)	No loans outstanding	No loans outstanding (1987)

Source: *A Few Words from the Canadian Banks About Loans to South Africa* (Taskforce on the Churches and Corporate Responsibility, May 1987).

the Toronto Dominion Bank had five and the Bank of Montreal had four.

Citing these figures, TCCR has accused the banks of flocking to Chile to profit from Pinochet's repressive régime. More recently, the banks have expressed growing reluctance to issue loans to developing countries like Chile because of the fear that they will not repay. However, Canadian banks are participating in an international plan to renegotiate Chile's existing debt to make it easier for Chile to repay.

When TCCR suggested that Canadian banks have a responsibility to attempt to persuade the Chilean régime to improve its human-rights record, senior bank managers replied that they have little bargaining power. According to TCCR, the managers said that "special considerations concerning human rights in Chile are difficult to advance, since non-rescheduling would lead to a total collapse and no one could force the régime to repay."[*]

The banks' record of investment in South Africa and Chile shows that they are avoiding new loans. In the case of the South African government and its agencies, the banks have imposed an outright ban. There is no ban on private-sector loans, but the banks are avoiding new loans for economic reasons, if not ethical ones.

If investment in countries with repressive régimes is an important ethical criterion for you (see chapter 3 for further discussion of ethical "screens"), you may want to consider the international lending record of the banks. However, at least one major Canadian ethical investment fund — the Investors Summa Fund — is satisfied that the banks do not support repressive régimes, one of its ethical criteria. In April 1987 all five of the major banks were included in its portfolio.

If you want further information on the investment record of the banks, you should write to the Taskforce on the Churches and Corporate Responsibility (address in appendix 3).

Labour Practices

Canadian banks in general, and many trust companies, are beginning to institute reform-minded policies on labour relations. The Bank of Nova Scotia, for instance, offers prorated benefits for part-time employees, a commitment that no employee will be discharged for technological change, and an employee ownership plan.

The Ethical Growth Fund, a Canadian mutual fund that screens investments for "progressive industrial relations," among other criteria, held shares in three banks in June 1987.

That said, the banks and many trust companies have been criticized heavily by the Canadian Labour Congress and affiliated unions for attempts to block the certification of bank employees and hard-line contract bargaining. For example, in 1987 the Canada Labour Relations Board imposed a settlement on the Canadian Imperial Bank of Commerce after a bitter strike with a union representing the bank's Visa workers.

"The CIBC's short-term plan was to keep the union impotent, with the long-term goal of operating its business without the encumbrance of collective bargaining," said the board in its report on the dispute. "In short, what we saw was the bank's uncompromising yet skillfully

[*] 1985-86 TCCR annual report

camouflaged rejection of the principles of the freedom of association upon which the [Canada Labour] Code is founded."

In another example, the Canadian Labour Congress called for a national boycott of Canada Trust in 1984, citing intransigent bargaining with a union representing Canada Trust employees in Cambridge, Ontario.

While generalizations about credit unions are difficult, the small size of most credit unions means that they do not have the impersonal labour relations typical of many financial institutions.

Community Relations

Do financial institutions serve the needs of businesses and individuals in communities? Are they sensitive to the special requirements of depressed communities? Do they support innovative or cooperatively owned businesses? Do financial institutions donate to community causes?

The answer to the questions of community support vary from institution to institution. However, because credit unions are locally based institutions, they need local borrowers for the money they raise in deposits. This means that, even if a credit union is located in a depressed community, it must find ways of lending deposit money in that community. This is not the case with larger institutions that can take deposits in one community and loan them in another.

"A bank can close a branch and there's no big trauma," says Gary Gillam of the Credit Union Central of Ontario. "A credit union can't pick up and leave. They don't have the luxury of picking up shop and going elsewhere. Because of this, they have a real interest in the restructuring of the economy and a real motivation to work closely with community leaders, community service organizations and their own members to ameliorate some of the consequences of the restructuring."

This said, it must still be recognized that the banks are the big lenders to small business, and small businesses provide a big proportion of jobs in communities. The Canadian Federation of Independent Business estimates there are 850,000 small businesses in Canada, 85 per cent of which use banks as their primary source of financing.

In addition, the banks are big contributors to charitable organizations. For example, the Bank of Montreal donates "to eligible and worthy causes, institutions or organizations whose work benefits the community at the local, regional or national level and also in foreign countries where the bank has significant branch offices or subsidiaries." The bank donates to United Way agencies, Big Brothers, Boy Scouts, Junior Achievement, YM/YWCAs, universities, health organizations and other charities.

Still, credit unions are the financial institution in the forefront of innovative and progressive solutions to local economic problems. The Desjardins group of *caisses populaires* in Quebec is very active in this area. In 1986 the group undertook a social audit — an accounting of its social impact — and found that its 324 affiliated *caisses* spent 7,576 working days on community programs in 1985. That represented about $1 million in salaries. In addition, members of boards of directors gave a total of 1,837 days' work to such projects. One of the community programs launched by the Desjardins federation in 1986 involved the promotion of so-called peoples' councils, bodies in which retired people would help young and unemployed people develop their own businesses.

Many English-language credit unions are undertaking similar projects, but two credit unions are especially well-known for their community development work — Bread and Roses Credit Union in Toronto, and CCEC Credit Union in Vancouver.

In 1986, Bread and Roses loaned $821,000 to local groups in Toronto, including four housing cooperatives, seven worker cooperatives or collectives, fifteen non-profit service groups, five arts organizations and seven media services. "Priority is given to loan applications related to financing for social justice projects or general community development," says Bread and Roses. "The credit union will not loan money for any projects which are perceived to exploit human beings or the environment."

CCEC (Community Congress for Economic Change) began in 1974 when a group of people active in consumer, daycare and housing groups found that they were having difficulty raising capital for their organizations. They founded CCEC to respond to this need. "Our encouragement and support of cooperative, democratic and self-help groups promotes responsible action in the areas of: racial and gender equality, conservation and social justice, as well as helping to provide for individual needs of food, shelter and employment. We keep your money working in your community."

Bigger credit unions are also making an impact. In 1986, Vancouver City Savings Credit Union established a seed-capital program to support individuals with ideas for business that showed potential and that would not be eligible for conventional financing. Graduates of local-college entrepreneur programs were given preference. Eight projects were funded in the first year.

Summarizing the Record

This all-too-brief rundown of the ethical record should be read with an eye to the history and social milieu of the three kinds of financial institutions. Canadian banks are world-scale institutions owned by thousands of shareholders and managed by executives who sit on the boards of some of the country's largest corporations. Similarly, Canada's largest trust companies are controlled by conglomerates with holdings in all sorts of industries. Only credit unions are owned and controlled by the customers who use them. While some financial institutions may satisfy certain social screens, ethical investors should ask whether they are satisfied with the ethical history of their institution and the role that it plays in the wider society.

CONSUMER ISSUES

With competition heating up between banks, trust companies and credit unions, two things are happening in the consumer banking market. The first trend is that financial institutions are introducing a greater variety of consumer services. Financial institutions have brought out treasury-bill savings accounts, which pay interest according to the weekly level on government of Canada treasury bills; flexible repayment options on personal loans and mortgages; and automatic teller machines, among other innovations. These services are generating new consumer business, a growing area of bank profits. In its 1986 report, the Royal reported that residential mortgages and consumer loans accounted for nearly 30 per cent of the bank's total loans, up from 22 per cent four years earlier.

The second major trend in the retail financial market spells bad news for consumers. Although bank customers can choose from an increasing range of services, financial institutions are raising their charges for these services and imposing charges on services that used to be free. An analysis by the Canadian Co-operative Credit Society, the national financial organization for credit unions and cooperatives, shows that the banks are taking higher revenues from their service charges to offset lower profits on their other operations. "Lingering loan problems in developing countries and in the Canadian energy sector have cut into banks' profitability," says an internal CCCS publication. "The banks' marketing strategy is now focused on development and promotion of retail products, and adherence to the 'user pay' philosophy that shifts most of the cost of providing a service to the user of that service."

The Royal reported that its income from service charges rose by 13 per cent in 1986 to $321 million, 11 per cent of its net income before expenses. The Bank of Montreal, Canada's second-largest financial institution, reported a whopping 27-per-cent increase in service-charge income to $235 million, 9 per cent of the bank's pre-expense net profit. And the Bank of Nova Scotia, ranked fourth-largest, reported a 26-per-cent increase in service-charge income to $94 million, 5.6 per cent of its pre-expense net income.

Consumer groups have become angered by such increases. The Consumers' Association of Canada is pressing the banks to publicize their service charges so that customers know exactly how much they will be charged.

With hundreds of credit unions in the country, generalizations about service fees are difficult. Each credit union sets its own policy according to member interest and local competition. However, the Canadian Co-operative Credit Society advises credit unions to look to member needs as well as credit union financial requirements. As it said in its internal publication:

> Because of their unique position as member-owned institutions, credit unions cannot and should not blindly adopt a strict "user pays" philosophy. Still, they cannot ignore the prevailing trend in the industry.... Credit unions must see service fees as an important source of revenue that can allow narrower margins, which contributes to the financial health of the credit union and enhances its ability to provide new and varied services.
>
> The other way to look at service fees is from a marketing perspective. If your competitors' fees are exorbitant compared to your own credit union's service fees, that's a good thing to shout about. Current members and potential members alike are bound to take notice.

Many credit unions are taking this advice to heart. A 1987 study of service fees in Quebec, conducted by Consumer Aid Services of Shawiningan, found that Desjardins-group *caisses populaires* provided services equivalent to the banks', but at about half the cost.

Accounts

As a consumer of financial services, you will need a saving, chequing or other type of account to do everyday banking. How do the various types of institutions stack up on accounts?

Savings accounts

True savings accounts do not offer chequing privileges. In order to withdraw money from them, you must make a withdrawal in person or through an automated teller machine. Interest in true savings accounts is calculated on your minimum monthly balance and paid twice a year.

These accounts have dropped in popularity since the introduction of daily-interest savings accounts, which calculate interest on your daily closing balance and pay interest monthly. Some institutions also offer more sophisticated accounts, such as the T-bill accounts mentioned earlier.

Not all credit unions offer sophisticated savings accounts, but certainly Canadians living in all major centres do have access to credit unions that offer such services. While credit unions have traditionally claimed that lower margins allowed them to pay higher interest on their savings accounts, this no longer seems to be the case. Falling interest rates in other sectors of the economy have squeezed the spread in interest rates between what credit unions and other financial institutions earn from borrowers and pay out to depositors.

"Within the credit-union context there still are shopping opportunities, but they're not as great as they used to be and they're not as frequent," says John Ellis, marketing director of the Credit Union Central of Ontario. Some closed-bond credit unions, such as employee credit unions, can offer higher interest to depositors because of lower operating costs, however. Often their offices are donated by the companies where the credit union is located, or employees work in the credit union on a volunteer basis.

Chequing Accounts

Regular chequing accounts pay no interest, but most institutions will return cheques and provide a monthly statement. Many charge a monthly fee. Many also charge for cheque processing or withdrawals. There are also chequing/savings accounts and daily-interest chequing accounts. Chequing/savings accounts pay interest, but at a lower rate than savings accounts. Daily-interest chequing accounts are growing in popularity for people who want the convenience of one account for their saving and chequing requirements.

Most credit unions offer chequing accounts, but because chequing accounts generally require full-time staff, some closed-bond credit unions in Ontario do not offer them. However, Canadians in major cities have access to credit unions offering chequing accounts.

Service Package Plans

These types of accounts are also growing in popularity. They generally operate from some type of chequing account, and permit free withdrawals and cheque processing, along with a variety of other services including money orders, traveller's cheques, overdraft protection and bill payments. They are ideal for people who write many cheques a month, or who need specialized services such as money orders or traveller's cheques each month. They also save on postage costs for paying utility and other types of bills.

Credit unions have been slow to offer service package plans. However, many credit unions already offer free unlimited chequing, so service package plans may not be as beneficial to members of these credit unions as they are to customers of a bank or trust company.

Investments

In addition to a basic bank account, many consumers of financial services will want an investment in which to place spare cash. Banks, trust companies and credit unions offer investments of various kinds that appeal to consumers who want a guaranteed rate of interest, and assurance that their principal is safe. These investments are guaranteed — within prescribed limits — by the Canada Deposit Insurance Corp. or provincial government credit-union-deposit insurance agencies.

These investments generally fall into two main categories: guaranteed investment certificates (GICs) or term deposits. Financial institutions require depositors to invest minimum amounts into these vehicles, unlike savings or chequing accounts. GICs are usually sold in terms of between one and five years, and can be redeemed before maturity only if the depositor foregoes interest. Term deposits are usually sold in terms of between thirty days and five years, and can usually be redeemed early but also at a penalty.

Many financial institutions also offer Canada Savings Bonds, which go on sale each year in October. These bonds have a set rate of interest and are guaranteed by the federal government.

For more sophisticated investors, some financial institutions offer mutual funds, which pool investments in the stock, mortgage or bond markets. Credit unions have access to mutual funds offered through Co-Operative Trust Co. of Canada, which is owned by the credit union system. Vancouver City Savings Credit Union also offers the Ethical Growth Fund, an ethical mutual fund. It is important to note that these are *not* guaranteed investments. (More on these investments in chapter 3).

A number of banks and trust companies also offer stock-brokerage services, an area off-limits to credit unions because of federal and provincial legislation.

From an ethical point of view, does it make any difference whether you purchase a term deposit or GIC from a credit union or from a bank?

Since credit unions do a greater proportion of their lending in the form of personal loans than banks or trust companies do, a deposit with a credit union has a greater likelihood than a deposit at another financial institution of ending up as this type of a loan. This is particularly the case if the deposit is for a relatively short term.

Long-term deposits are usually matched with long-term loans, such as mortgages. Most credit unions offer mortagages to their members. Some other credit unions take long-term deposit money and turn it over to the Co-Operative Trust Co. of Canada. Ethical investors may be interested in asking their credit unions whether they have an agreement with Co-Op Trust, which does more lending to cooperative housing projects than any other financial institution in Canada.

If your credit union deposit supports the financing of Co-Op Trust, you can be sure that a good proportion of your deposit is being used to finance socially useful housing projects. (For a discussion of the ethical dimensions of guaranteed RRSP investments, see the next chapter).

By comparison, banks, trust companies and insurance companies lend a tiny proportion of their long-term money to cooperative housing projects, favouring privately held mortgages instead.

Credit
There are four main sources of credit available to consumers — credit cards, personal loans, lines of credit and mortgages. Internationally-known Visa and MasterCard credit cards are issued by banks and trust companies and some credit unions. Many other credit unions offer the MasterCard II payment card instead. A MasterCard II payment card directly debits your credit-union account instead of extending credit as

in conventional MasterCard or Visa accounts. This is useful if wish to pay for purchases directly from your account. In addition, if your credit union offers personal lines of credit, you can use this as a way of getting credit from your payment card.

A line of credit is a kind of standby loan, a credit limit that you are able to draw upon for emergencies or big-ticket purchases. A secured line of credit is backed by a pledge of your assets, such as your home or Canada Savings Bonds. Secured lines have lower interest rates than unsecured lines. You are charged interest only on the money you actually borrow from the line of credit.

Since lines of credit generally have much lower interest rates than credit-card accounts, a line of credit matched with a payment card gives you the convenience of using a card for payment, but at lower rates of interest. In order to do this, you simply assign your payment-card debits and your line of credit to the same account.

Credit unions favour the payment-card system because it imposes less of a credit risk on the credit union itself and encourages better credit practices among members. Payment cards and lines of credit are still not widely available among credit unions in all provinces, however.

Personal loans, available from all three types of institutions, are granted to borrowers who can show they have enough income or assets to cover their payments. It is generally easier to borrow money from a credit union than from a bank or trust company. This is particularly the case in provinces such as Ontario, where credit unions are allowed to garnishee wages if a borrower goes into long-term default on a loan. Only credit unions have this right. This means that credit unions can issue loans to lower- income borrowers or those with little net worth because they can draw on the borrower's own wages if he or she neglects to pay. Also, because most credit unions are smaller than banks and trust companies, it is generally easier to develop a personal relationship with a credit-union manager — an important feature if you have difficulty meeting your payments.

This ease of borrowing is especially important to single women, who have traditionally had trouble getting consumer credit from banks and trust companies. Credit unions have been aware of this problem, and many have taken special action to offer credit to women. The Ottawa Women's Credit Union has a policy of lending money to low-income women or women on welfare, family-allowance payments or unemployment insurance. VanCity says it was one of the first financial institutions to qualify women for credit on the basis of their own earnings.

Credit unions also compete favourably with banks and trust companies on mortgages for home financing. As with personal loans, if you have a low income or a low net worth, it will likely be easier to get a mortgage from a credit union than from a bank. However, some credit unions, especially closed-bond credit unions with a restricted membership, have difficulty in raising enough mortgage money to meet the demand for loans. These credit unions often have to place their mortgage applicants on a waiting list.

It may also be easier to arrange flexible mortgage-payment options at a credit union, although banks and trust companies adopted these options after they were pioneered by credit unions.

In October 1981, amid skyhigh interest rates, St. Willibrord Community Credit Union in London, Ontario, offered an innovative payment plan. By reducing traditional monthly payments to smaller, weekly chunks, synchronizing them with salary payments and making fifty-two weekly payments rather than twelve monthly ones, members effectively paid down more of their mortgage principal every year. This has allowed mortgage-holders to cut years off the time needed to repay their mortgages and provided big savings in interest payments. Other financial institutions have adopted this plan.

Automated Teller Machines

Of all the innovations introduced by the financial industry in the last few years, the one that has probably had the greatest impact on personal banking is automatic teller machines. Because they are small, discrete units, credit unions are behind the banks but ahead of trust companies in the introduction of ATM banking. Small credit unions generally cannot afford to install ATM equipment, and the small number of branches operated by small credit unions discourage members from using ATMs even if they are installed.

However, local credit unions in Saskatchewan and Ontario with ATMs were the first to connect to the Interac network, which allows members to do banking from about four thousand machines at bank and trust company branches across Canada. *Caisses populaires* with ATMs in Quebec are also members of the system through the Desjardins group. Large credit unions in rural areas have often been the only financial institutions to bring ATM banking to their communities.

Trust Services and Insurance

As mentioned previously, the Canadian credit union and co-operative system owns its own trust company, the Co-Operative Trust Co. of Canada. Co-Op Trust offers a wide range of trust services, including GICs, registered retirement savings plans (RRSPs), registered retirement income funds (RRIFs) and trusteeship services. Individuals may contact Co-Op Trust directly or through their credit union, if it has a referral arrangement. In the Maritimes, League Savings and Mortgage, a trust company controlled by Maritime credit unions, offers a wide range of trust services, including guaranteed investments, RRSPs and mortgages. (Addresses for these companies are in appendix 1).

Credit-union members can also receive a wide range of insurance services through CUMIS (Credit Union Member Insurance Societies), founded in 1935 by credit-union organizers who were unable to find a suitable commercial insurance company. CUMIS offers term life insurance, which insures you for between $50,000 and $500,000 for a term of five years. Other insurance services are also available. You can contact CUMIS by writing to the address in appendix 1, or through some credit unions. Property and casualty insurance, and other types of insurance, are available from The Co-Operators Group Ltd. Although there are no official connections between individual credit unions and The Co-Operators, the company is owned by 36 cooperative and cooperatively-oriented organizations. You can obtain information by writing to the address in appendix 1.

In Quebec, the Desjardins group of *caisses populaires* offers insurance and trust services through two affiliated companies. For information, write to the Desjardins federation at the address in appendix 1.

Summarizing Consumer Issues

In terms of bank accounts and basic investments, the banks, trust companies and credit unions are slugging it out to offer customized services. Marketplace competition is changing from an emphasis on interest rates to an emphasis on customer service and service charges. Each type of institution offers an array of services, and in keeping with the trend to higher service charges, there are a variety of different fees charged. Credit unions generally come out ahead on service fees even if interest rates are similar to the other institutions.

For many borrowers, credit unions often are the only place where a mortgage or consumer loan can be negotiated. Terms are often better at credit unions, but this is more often the case in payment options than interest rates.

Credit unions are pioneering the introduction of new services to the financial market, but they are not as competitive as the banks in terms of ATMs. However, credit unions are working to bring their system up to par with the banks.

Through links with cooperatively-owned trust and insurance companies, many credit unions are able to refer members to other progressive financial institutions that can offer a wide range of personal financial services.

SECURITY OF DEPOSIT

For generations Canadians believed that their money was completely safe in a bank, trust company or credit union. That faith has been shaken with the disturbing collapse of more than a dozen trust and loan companies since 1980, and the failures of the Canadian Commercial Bank and the Northland Bank in 1985. As a result, Canadians are becomingly increasingly concerned about the issue of the security of their deposits.

Are deposits in a credit union safe? Are they as safe in a credit union as they are in a bank or trust company?

The short answer to these questions is simple. As the Canadian Co-operative Credit Society states, "No member has ever lost a cent of his/her deposits in a credit union." The same claim cannot be made about other financial institutions. In 1980, for example, about sixteen hundred depositors lost a total of $24 million with the failure of Toronto-based Argosy Financial Group of Canada Ltd. More recently, financial experts estimate that depositors in Alberta-based Principal Group Ltd. could lose $10 million from the 1987 collapse of the company. While banks are well-secured, there were depositors who lost money when the Home Bank of Canada went down in 1923. The long answer to these questions about security of deposits is more complex. While the relatively small size of credit unions gives them less financial solidity than the mammoth chartered banks, the regulatory and financial backstops in the credit-union system are designed to identify problem credit unions, provide assistance and merge them with other credit unions, if necessary. The system has been put to the test during the last few years, when many Western credit unions struggled under recession conditions. Several large mergers took place, and the system appears to be stronger now than when the recession in Western Canada began in the early 1980s.

For customers of banks and trust companies, the most important protection is the deposit guarantee provided by the Canada Deposit Insurance Corp (CDIC). CDIC, a federal government corporation, was established in 1967 to protect depositors and to ensure that consumers have confidence in their financial institutions. Its operations are funded by an annual premium paid by member institutions.

CDIC insures deposits up to $60,000 in banks and federally incorporated trust and loan companies, as well as insuring deposits made outside Quebec in provincially chartered trust and loan companies. This includes all the major banks and trust companies, and most of the smaller ones as well. The only stipulation on this insurance is that the deposit must have a maturity of five years or less. Investment certificates or other deposits of greater than five years are not insured.

Deposit protection in credit unions is actually higher in most provinces. For credit unions, deposits are insured by provincial deposit-insurance corporations. In all provinces but one — Ontario — there is no specific ceiling placed on the amount of the deposit that is guaranteed. In Ontario, the guarantee is the same as the CDIC guarantee — $60,000. In order to receive higher protection, credit-union depositors in Ontario should open more than one account and keep a maximum of only $60,000 in each account.

Unlike CDIC, the provincial deposit-insurance corporations are empowered to take an active role in the supervision of credit unions. This means that these organizations can monitor the operations of individual credit unions, provide advice and direction where required and, in extreme circumstances, assume temporary management to rectify problems.

This supervisory role has been put to the test during the last few years. Perhaps the most impressive turnaround concerns the Société d'entraide économique du Québec Inc., a group of about seventy-five credit unions in Quebec. The "Caisse d'entraide," as it is known, is a federation of credit unions separate from the larger Desjardins group. In 1981, the Caisse d'entraide almost collapsed when depositors withdrew their money in a panic following allegations of mismanagement and conflicts of interest. As part of a recovery plan, several local credit unions formerly affiliated with the Caisse d'entraide joined the Desjardins group, some were closed and others were merged. By October 1986, Caisse d'entraide chairman Robert Arcand was able to claim a "spectacular recovery" in the federation's operations, including a profit of $7.1 million for the year.Credit unions in Calgary and Edmonton are also on the road to better financial health since they were formally merged in March 1987. The Alberta Credit Union Stabilization Corporation — the provincial deposit-insurance fund — began managing forty- seven troubled credit unions in 1984 and 1985 after they started racking up losses. More than $300 million worth of foreclosed properties were turned over to the stabilization fund in return for $355 million in debentures. The fund will sell the properties gradually during the next few years to recoup the money paid through the debentures.

In order to set the credit unions on a better footing, the stabilization fund ordered credit unions to merge in Edmonton and Calgary. While the membership of the credit unions ultimately held the decision on whether to merge, the stabilization corporation backed up its order with the threat that it would liquidate the credit unions if they did not comply. By early 1987 seven credit unions in Calgary were merged into a new institution called First Calgary Financial Savings and Credit Union. With 120,000 members, the new institution is one of the largest credit unions in the country. At the time of the merger, plans were in place to introduce new credit services, make its lending more flexible and otherwise compete better with the banks and trust companies.

In addition to the deposit guarantees and regulatory powers of the deposit-insurance corporations, credit unions are helped in overcoming temporary cash shortages through their provincial credit-union centrals. Among the English-language credit unions, the centrals hold $1.8 billion available to local credit unions in need of ready cash. The Canadian Co-operative Credit Society, the organization of provincial centrals, has assets of more than $1 billion, half of which is available to the centrals.

HOW TO JOIN

With fifteen hundred credit unions and fourteen hundred *caisses populaires* across the country, many cities and rural areas in Canada are served by more than one cooperative credit institution. Anyone wishing to join a credit union should first determine which credit union best matches his or her style, philosophy and needs.

Not all credit unions are open to all members within a community. Since some credit unions serve a particular industry, profession or ethnic group, you may not be able to join unless you fit a particular category. Otherwise, membership is open to anyone in a particular community.

Credit unions are generally listed in the Yellow Pages of telephone directories, but a better way of obtaining a list of credit unions in your area is to contact the credit-union central for your province. A list of the addresses and telephone numbers for these centrals can be found in appendix 1.

Once you obtain a list of local credit unions, it is possible to call or write for a copy of their annual reports. Annual reports provide information to prospective members including the types of service offered, the history and size of the credit union and whether it has any special programs, such as community economic investments. While interest rates and service charges probably will not be included in the annual report, you can ask for a rate bulletin to provide the specifics.

After choosing a credit union, you must purchase a share, which ranges between $5 and $25. The share entitles you to membership in the credit union and gives you access to all its services.

2

RRSPs — THE PLACE TO BEGIN INVESTING

For Canadians with a social conscience, the RRSP (Registered Retirement Savings Plan) can present a moral dilemma. From a consumer point of view, it is a good way to maximize returns on savings stowed away in a long-term investment. Not only does the RRSP-holder save on taxes each year but the RRSP fund itself accumulates interest, dividends or capital without being taxed.

But there is a problem with RRSPs for Canadians concerned about the distribution of income between rich and poor. Like many other aspects of our tax system, RRSPs provide greater benefits for those with greater income. As a result, it seems hard to justify the RRSP on social grounds considering that the government is indirectly subsidizing people with higher incomes, who are less in need of help for their retirement years than low-income-earners.

Does this mean that socially conscious investors and savers should tear up their RRSP certificates? The answer is no.

The fact is that the RRSP provides an excellent means for people of moderate income to express their social values with their money. The RRSP provides the tax incentive that makes saving possible for thousands of middle-income Canadians. Once you have accumulated a nestegg of a few thousand dollars with the help of the tax system, you can put that RRSP toward investments that match your financial goals and express your social values.

WHAT IS AN RRSP?

Started in 1957, with a change to the Income Tax Act, RRSPs have become enormously popular. By the end of 1986, about 3.1 million Canadians were registered as RRSP plan-holders, and the total assets covered under RRSPs amounted to more than $46 billion.

Registered retirement savings plans are — in accountancy lingo — a tax shelter. This means that they protect a certain amount of income from taxation. The sheltered income is placed in an investment vehicle where it earns interest, generates dividends or the capital itself grows in value. Regardless of how income is generated from the investment, you do not have to declare it as income on your tax return as long as it remains in the RRSP.

The income set aside within the RRSP is not sheltered from taxation for all time; it is merely deferred. For typical RRSP-savers, the taxation is deferred until retirement, when income is lower. Deferring taxation until retirement or another low-income period carries important benefits to taxpayers. But you do not have to wait until retirement to make use of your RRSP funds, a point that will be explained in more detail in this chapter and in chapter 6, which discusses how to take time off from your job.

The idea is to save taxes now — when you are working — and draw on your RRSP funds when you are not working. Under Canada's system of taxation, income is taxed according to a "ladder" of rates. Your lowest block of income is taxed at a very low rate, the next block of income is taxed at a higher rate, and so on (more on this in chapter 4 on taxation). Since your marginal rate should be very low when you retire, you should not be hit with a big tax bill when you draw on your RRSP savings.

There are no regulations prohibiting you from drawing on RRSP funds when your income is relatively high, but the tax penalty is severe. Unless you have a lower-than-normal income when you withdraw RRSP funds, the RRSP money will be taxed at a relatively high marginal rate.

RRSP contributions — which must be made by March 1 in order to qualify as a deduction for the preceding tax year — can generate significant yearly tax savings. For example, a taxpayer with a marginal rate of 35 per cent who contributes $3,500 to an RRSP will save himself or herself $1,125 in taxes. If that taxpayer contributes $3,500 a year for thirty years in a tax-free registered plan earning 13-per-cent interest annually, he or she will be able to retire with a fund containing more than $1 million. Of course, it must be kept in mind that thirty years of inflation will cut heavily into the spending power of $1 million in 1987 dollars.

Table 3

RRSP Growth Rate:
$3,500 a Year at Various Interest Rates over Thirty Years

% return	1 yr.	5 yrs.	10 yrs.	20 yrs.	30 yrs.
5	3,675	20,307	46,224	121,517	244,163
7	3,745	21,537	51,743	153,528	353,756
9	3,815	22,832	57,961	195,176	520,013
11	3,885	24,195	64,965	249,428	773,196
13	3,955	25,629	72,850	320,145	1,159,603
15	4,025	27,138	81,722	412,335	1,749,849
17	4,095	28,724	91,700	532,485	2,651,263
19	4,165	30,390	102,912	688,966	4,026,356
21	4,235	32,140	115,505	892,562	6,120,213

Table 4

RRSP Growth Rate: $7,500 a Year at Various Interest Rates
over Thirty Years

% return	1 yr.	5 yrs.	10 yrs.	20 yrs.	30 yrs.
5	7,875	43,514	99,051	260,394	523,206
7	8,025	46,150	110,877	328,989	758,048
9	8,175	48,925	124,202	418,234	1,114,314
11	8,325	51,846	139,211	534,489	1,656,849
13	8,475	54,920	156,107	686,024	2,484,863
15	8,625	58,153	175,120	883,576	3,749,677
17	8,775	61,551	196,500	1,141,039	5,681,278
19	8,925	65,122	220,527	1,476,356	8,627,906
21	9,075	68,872	247,510	1,912,632	13,114,742

One of the reasons that financial planners recommend RRSPs is because government retirement benefits are not expected to provide adequate income for a good portion of retired Canadians in the future.

Working Canadians who retire are eligible to receive Canada Pension Plan (CPP) or Quebec Pension Plan payments (QPP). In 1987, the maximum monthly payment under these plans was $521.52. Retirees are eligible for additional payments under the Old Age Security plan, and low-income retirees are eligible for the Guaranteed Income Supplement. However, economists estimate that these plans cannot provide enough income to maintain people in their pre-retirement style of life.

In a 1979 paper prepared for a national conference on incomes, Michael Wolfson, a tax advisor for the federal Finance Department, estimated that the upper 50 to 70 per cent of income-earners are likely to suffer a income drop of 25 to 50 per cent in retirement if no individual retirement provisions are made.

Moreover, the "greying" of the Baby Boom generation born between 1946 and 1959 will place a rising burden on younger people to pay any shortfall between CPP premiums and pension payouts. The CPP is funded from contributions made by employers and employees and from interest earned on investments of excess revenue. Under reforms begun on January 1, 1987, employer and employee contributions are scheduled to rise from 2 per cent of pensionable earnings in 1988 to 2.3 per cent in 1991. This level will be reviewed every five years thereafter. It is uncertain how far a shrinking generation of workers will agree to finance a growing generation of retirees.

It is becoming increasingly important for people to plan for their retirement early in their lifetime if they want to avoid a big drop in income after they say goodbye to their job. Flexible retirement ages and the growth of part-time work may take some of the urgency out of the problem, since it is likely that many Canadians in the future will continue to work into their late sixties and seventies. But retirement savings plans can give people the freedom to choose the kind of lifestyle they want to maintain in retirement. Further, with a large retirement fund to draw upon, retirees can decide whether they want to continue working. Employment will not be forced on them by simple lack of money.

SHOULD EVERYONE HAVE AN RRSP?

The question of whether you should have an RRSP depends largely on your income and other details of your financial situation. Certainly for middle-age people who have paid off big debts such as mortgages, and upper-and middle-income people, the consensus among financial planners is clear: RRSPs provide indisputable benefits. The benefits for younger people, who tend to carry a higher debt load, or for low-income people who receive a lower tax benefit, are less clear.

The previously mentioned Wolfson study concluded that, for the top 20 per cent of income-earners, RRSPs are more attractive — in after-tax rates of return — than an owner-occupied house. However, Wolfson also concluded that the most attractive form of saving for the bottom half of income-earners is a house. For the bottom 20 per cent, RRSPs actually represent the worst form of saving when compared with bank saving, house saving, stock dividends and capital gains.

To know where you fall within this scale of income-earners, here is a rough guide. The federal government's statistics on 1984 income taxes (the latest year available) show that about 15.6 million Canadians filed with Revenue Canada. The bottom 20 per cent of these taxfilers had a total income of $5,000 or less. The bottom 50 per cent included nearly everyone earning less than $14,500. The top 20 per cent of income-earners had a total income above $30,000. These figures may come as a surprise to people who think of themselves as "middle-income" earners, but they include taxfilers who were homemakers, students, part-time workers and other low-income Canadians.

This guide suggests that people earning $30,000 or more should certainly have an RRSP, while the benefits of an RRSP are less clear for people earning less than $30,000. However, since it is becoming increasingly difficult to purchase a house, especially in large cities, an RRSP is still an attractive way of saving for millions of middle-income Canadians.

The problem becomes even more vexing when you consider that it is better to start an RRSP earlier than later. The longer an RRSP fund can accumulate interest, dividends or capital growth, the bigger the fund will be when the time comes to draw on it for retirement. Consider this hypothetical example. A fairly typical RRSP plan-holder can manage to save $3,500 a year in an investment earning 9 per cent a year. If the plan-holder begins the plan at age thirty-five, he or she could retire at age sixty-five with a retirement savings fund of $520,013. If that plan-holder had waited until age forty-five to start contributing, the retirement fund would only amount to $195,176.

Depending on your individual financial circumstances, it might make more sense to wait before opening an RRSP, or to suspend contributions for a few years. In other cases, it might make more sense to combine RRSP saving with other types of saving, including payments into a mortgage.

HOW MUCH CAN I CONTRIBUTE?

Here are Ottawa's current rules defining how much Canadians can contribute toward their RRSPs. Contributions must be made by March 1 in order to be deductible for the previous tax year. If you exceed these contribution limits, you are subject to a tax penalty of one per cent per month on any excess.

For the 1987 and 1988 Tax Years:
- If you are like most Canadians, who are not members of a registered pension plan (RRP) or a deferred profit sharing plan, you can contribute up to $7,500 or 20 per cent (whichever is less) of your earned income. If you are a member of a registered pension plan or deferred profit sharing plan, you can contribute up to $3,500 or 20 per cent (whichever is less) of your earned income, minus your annual contributions to the RPP.
- For most Canadians, earned income is your salary and wages (the earnings from Box C of your T4 slip) minus certain expenses, such as unemployment insurance premiums.
- Other Canadians may also add the following to their earned income: tips, retirement allowances, royalties, alimony or maintenance payments received, profit sharing or stock option benefits, payments from a collapsed RRSP or deferred profit sharing plan, business and rental income. However, if you have earned any of these forms of income, you may have to subtract business or rental losses and other specified items.

For Future Years:
- If you are like most Canadians, who are not members of a registered pension plan or deferred profit sharing plan, you can contribute 18 per cent of your earned income to an RRSP, up to certain maximums, which are set out below. Following changes announced by Finance Minister Michael Wilson in October, 1986, and reaffirmed in the 1987 White Paper on taxation, these amounts will be reduced if you are a member of a registered pension plan or deferred profit sharing plan. The actual amounts to be deducted are based on complex formulations and, in an effort to assist taxpayers, Revenue Canada will calculate your contribution limit for you based on information received from your employer and will send a notice of this limit to you near the end of 1989 and subsequent years.

- Future maximums:1989 — $ 8,500
  - 1990 — $10,500
  - 1991 — $11,500
  - 1992 — $12,500
  - 1993 — $13,500
  - 1994 — $14,500
  - 1995 — $15,500
- Starting in 1989, people who do not use their allowable RRSP contribution will be able to carry it forward as much as seven years. That way, if you suspend contributions for a few years, you will be able to make them up later.

RRSPs AND RETIREMENT PLANNING

Your economic strategy for retirement planning hinges on a number of factors including your age, your personal "comfort level," the knowledge and time you have for managing your financial affairs and the size of your RRSP fund. All of these factors will help to determine the kind of RRSP investment that is best for you. At the same time, these factors will constrain the ethical choices open to you.

RRSP investments have differing ethical implications, as well as differing financial implications. The ethical dimensions of these choices will be explored later in this chapter. In order to make the best decision, however, you will have to be mindful of both financial and ethical considerations.

Finally, you should consider whether you want to contribute to the plan of your spouse, and whether or not it makes sense to borrow to help you finance your RRSP.

Age and Comfort Level

Not surprisingly, one of the most important factors in determining your retirement-planning strategy is your age.

Age is important because, as you grow older, you have fewer income-earning years until retirement. It becomes imperative, as you approach retirement, to minimize the risk to your assets. This is known as conservation of capital. It seems like an obvious point, but many financial planners tell stories of clients in their fifties who are desperately attempting to strike it rich in the stock market because they have not taken action to build a nestegg earlier in their lives.

Bob Quart, manager of trust services for Vancouver City Savings Credit Union, puts it this way: "I think somebody who is seventy-five years old should really think twice about investing in a growth fund. They should have done it when they were forty-five, unless they're investing funds that they don't need for living purposes and they can pass on to another generation. Certainly they shouldn't be [risking] funds that are required for emergencies."

Conversely, younger people do not need to be as concerned about capital conservation because they have decades of earning years ahead of them. If they lose money on an investment early in life, it is not a disaster. Similarly, if they have money invested in a cyclical type of investment that then takes a downward turn, they have plenty of years left in which that investment can take an upturn.

The importance of this for RRSPs is that younger people can afford to take risks with their RRSP money, while older people should place their RRSP funds in safe investments. Younger people should consider placing RRSP money in mutual funds, which pool investors' capital in stock-market investments, or in the stock market itself. Older people should stick to guaranteed investments, such as term deposits, treasury bills or Canada Savings Bonds.

Perhaps even more important than your age is your "investment comfort level." It does not make sense — even if you are only twenty-five — to invest in the stock market if you are uncomfortable with the decision. Your psychological well-being should not be sacrificed for what an investment adviser thinks is a good plan of action. In the end, it is this psychological factor that determines what investments should be made.

Knowledge and Time
Some RRSP investments require a great deal of sophisticated stock-market knowledge, backed up by daily readings of the business press. Other RRSP investments can be made in the spring and left alone until the next RRSP season rolls around.

While ethical investors will want to spend enough time satisfying themselves that they have chosen an RRSP investment that fits their ethical criteria, they may not be willing to spend a lot of time monitoring the financial performance of that investment.

Again, as with older investors, people who do not want to spend a lot of time on their investments should generally stick to guaranteed RRSP vehicles.

The Size of Your Fund

For most RRSP investors, the size of your RRSP fund will not be an important factor in choosing an investment. However, for a minority of RRSP investors, fund size is a critical factor. If you choose to invest in a guaranteed investment, the size of your fund is not important since most financial institutions will allow you to deposit your RRSP free of charge. Many mutual funds charge a fee, but the fee is usually a percentage of the amount you invest. If you choose stock-market investments, you should be sure to have a sizeable plan (financial advisers recommend at least $10,000). This is because you will have to pay a fee of usually about $100 a year for the self-directed RRSP required to trade in stocks. You will want to be sure that your RRSP is large enough to earn sufficient income to cover the cost of this fee.

Self-directed RRSPs will be discussed in greater detail later in this chapter.

Spousal RRSPs

In considering your RRSP and retirement needs, one of the most important things to consider — especially if you are nearing retirement — is how the income of you and your spouse will be taxed after retirement. If it looks as if one spouse is going to be taxed at a very high rate and one spouse is going to be taxed at a very low rate, it makes sense to take action now to equalize your retirement income as much as possible so that the household income will be taxed at a moderate rate.

You can do this with a spousal RRSP. A spousal plan is an RRSP in which a person contributes to the RRSP of his or her spouse. The total you are allowed to contribute toward your spouse's RRSP and deduct from your income cannot exceed the amount that you would normally contribute to your own plan. If you have already contributed toward your own plan, the total of the contribution to your plan and your spouse's plan cannot exceed your annual contribution limit.

The benefit of spousal RRSPs comes in retirement. If one spouse in a couple has worked most of his or her life, while the other has stayed at home, the one who has worked will have a large RRSP on retirement, while the stay-at-home spouse will have a relatively small RRSP. This income difference can be aggravated if the working spouse is also able to collect a company pension and/or investment income. Such a situation would mean that one spouse would be taxed at a very high marginal rate, say 50 per cent, while the other is taxed at a relatively low rate.

If the working spouse contributes to the non-working spouse's RRSP before retirement, the chances are greater that retirement income will be equalized. This means that the household income will be taxed at a lower rate.

Couples must carefully consider the effects of cashing in a spousal RRSP, however. Under the Income Tax Act, if the non-contributing spouse cashes in his or her plan, Revenue Canada will consider any contributions made by the contributing spouse in the last year and the previous two years to be taxable in the hands of the contributing spouse. There are special rules in the case of a marriage breakdown.

Spousal RRSPs do not constrain ethical investment choices because the same sort of ethical choices have to be made with spousal RRSPs as with individual RRSPs.

Borrowing for an RRSP

Like many Canadians who frantically try to make the March 1 deadline for RRSP contributions, you may find it hard to raise the necessary cash. Does it make sense for you to borrow the money to contribute?

While interest expenses incurred on loans to finance the purchase of stocks or bonds is deductible from your income (see chapter 4 on taxation), interest on loans for contributions to an RRSP is not deductible. This means that you may have to pay 12- or 13-per-cent interest for an RRSP that will return only 10 per cent. However, it may still be worth your while to borrow to finance your contribution.

Do not forget that a few years' delay in contributing to an RRSP when you are young can make an enormous difference to your final retirement fund. The best strategy to capitalize on a borrowed RRSP contribution is to use part or all of your tax refund to help pay the loan you took out for the contribution. Most personal loans can be negotiated on an open basis, so you can arrange with your credit union or bank manager to repay the loan in full when you receive your tax refund.

OTHER USES OF RRSPs

While an RRSP is normally considered for use in retirement, many Canadians are using RRSP savings to tide them over any period in which their income is reduced. Once an RRSP is cashed, the institution holding it is required to withhold a portion of the money for tax.

Still, the fund can come in handy if you quit your job or get laid off, or take a leave of absence.

The essential point to remember is that the tax penalty on your RRSP is minimal if your income is unusually low. In fact, if you have a very small income, you may have some tax deductions that are being wasted because you do not have sufficient income to make use of them. In this case, an RRSP cash-in represents the best use of those funds from an immediate tax point of view. The disadvantage, of course, is that you are lowering the future growth potential of your RRSP by withdrawing funds for use now. (See chapter 6 for further tips on taking time off work)

RRSP INVESTMENTS

Once you make the decision to purchase an RRSP, the next choice you have to make is where to purchase that RRSP and what kind of vehicle to invest in. Credit unions, banks, trust companies, insurance companies, mutual-fund dealers and stock brokers offer RRSPs. You can also set up a self-directed RRSP to purchase a large number of different types of investments from different institutions.

The list of "qualified investments" that are eligible for RRSPs under federal regulations covers a wide range of vehicles, including guaranteed deposits with credit unions, banks and trust companies, or other guaranteed investments such as government bonds and treasury bills. It also includes mutual funds and a variety of securities, such as stocks, bonds and debentures. Special qualified investments include debt obligations or shares in certain cooperatives or credit unions, shares in certain private corporations, annuity contracts, life-insurance policies and mortgages (including your own).

One important stipulation on these investments is that 90 per cent of the value of any particular plan must be locked away in Canadian investments. The federal government wants to ensure that tax-assisted Canadian savings are invested in Canada.

These investments leave a great deal of scope for ethical-investment choices. Generally, the legal constraints on RRSP investments are not important as far as ethical investors are concerned. Specific "non-qualified" investments are gold and silver bars, commodity futures, personal property (such as works of art), real estate and debt obligations of companies whose shares are listed only on foreign stock exchanges. These are generally speculative investments, which add little growth to the economy. Many ethical investors would avoid these on social grounds, even if they were legally permitted to use RRSP money to invest in them.

Each of the qualified investments, and each of the institutions authorized to offer RRSPs, pose ethical choices for investors. We should examine them in more detail.

- *Guaranteed investments.* These are backed by the federal government or deposit-insurance agencies, and include savings accounts, Canada Savings Bonds, GICs and term deposits. They are the safest type of RRSP investment and are fairly liquid (can be turned into cash without a great penalty.) The disadvantage is that they have no possibility for capital growth.
- *Mutual funds.* These are funds that pool a number of investments to maximize the return to the investor while minimizing risk. They are offered by banks, trust companies, insurance companies, mutual-fund dealers and stock brokers. There are a number of funds available to RRSP investors that screen investments according to ethical criteria. Professional fund managers are paid a fee to supervise the investments in the fund and to buy and sell investments at opportune times. Riskier than guaranteed investments, they carry the potential for capital growth.
- *Stocks and other securities.* Generally riskier than mutual funds. However, they permit greater freedom than mutual funds or guaranteed investments from financial and ethical viewpoints.
- *Special investments.* These have a variety of financial and ethical impacts, and should be carefully considered. Some may even require the advice of a lawyer.

ETHICAL CONSIDERATIONS

Guaranteed Investments

The most common types of guaranteed RRSPs are savings accounts, term deposits, guaranteed-investments certificates and Canada Savings Bonds.

As explained in the previous chapter on saving and borrowing, if you place money in a long-term deposit, your financial institution will attempt to match that money with a long-term loan or mortgage. The same is true with deposits or guaranteed investments registered as RRSPs.

While credit unions, banks and trust companies are all heavily involved in the residential mortgage market, many credit unions offer
one distinct difference for ethical investors: they are also involved in a
big way in cooperative and social housing projects.

Many credit unions have an agreement with the Co-operative Trust
Company of Canada, a federal trust firm controlled by the credit-union
system, to manage RRSP money raised locally. By pooling small
amounts of RRSP funds raised in hundreds of credit unions across
Canada, Co-op Trust has been able to form a sizeable pool of capital
to direct toward housing projects that are considered to be outside the
normal business of the banks and trust companies. As a result, Co-op
Trust has become the largest lender to cooperative housing in the
country, and this form of lending now makes up the bulk of Co-op
Trust's mortgage business. Not many credit unions promote this fact,
but Bread and Roses in Toronto actively uses its Co-op Trust connection to attract socially conscious investors. Bread and Roses promises
RRSP investors that "the greater part of your RRSP investment" will
be invested in cooperative housing mortgages by Co-op Trust.

Credit unions that offer RRSPs through Co-Op Trust generally
offer two types of plans: 1) a guaranteed fixed term available for between one and five years; and 2) a variable-rate plan in which the interest rate fluctuates with market conditions.

Co-op Trust is not the only cooperative financial institution in the
country that directs RRSP money toward cooperative housing projects.
League Savings and Mortgage, a federal trust company owned by the
credit unions of Atlantic Canada, accepts RRSP money directly and
through local credit unions in the Atlantic provinces. The company has
assets of $175 million, part of which is loaned out to innovative hous-
ing projects in rural areas of the Atlantic provinces.

The company has helped to finance programs to replace worn-out
houses for rural families, homes for battered women, community
economic development projects on Cape Breton Island and a number
of projects for non-profit groups.

While bankers may consider this kind of lending somewhat risky,
League Savings and Mortgage has a delinquency rate of only about 0.5
per cent. It also has one of the lowest loss ratios of all National Housing Act-approved lenders in Canada. In addition, as a member of the
CDIC, League Savings insures its debentures (similar to GICs) and
deposits up to $60,000.

You can obtain RRSP information from Co-Op Trust or League Savings by writing to the addresses listed in appendix 1. Both companies offer RRSPs directly to the public and through some credit unions.

Many individual credit unions also help to finance social housing projects. By the end of 1986, Vancouver City Savings Credit Union, for example, had sixty-two loans worth $78 million for construction of housing for senior citizens, the disabled and cooperatives.

RRSP deposits at credit unions, banks and trust companies are subject to the same deposit protection as non-registered deposits. (Deposit protection is discussed further in chapter 1)

If you want to know whether your credit union directs at least a portion of its RRSP money to social housing programs, or participates in social housing programs through credit-union- controlled trust companies, just ask your manager. If it does not, your inquiry might spark a new initiative.

Mutual Funds

Mutual funds are becoming an increasingly popular choice for RRSP-holders who want capital-growth opportunities without the hassles of managing stocks themselves. While the federal dividend tax credit and capital-gains exemption give large tax advantages to stocks and stock-based mutual funds held outside of an RRSP, many investors want to invest their RRSP money in a mutual fund to achieve capital growth. For many Canadians, an RRSP is the only sizeable investment they own, and they want it to grow as quickly as possible.

All four ethical mutual funds in Canada available to individual investors are eligible to be registered as an RRSP (descriptions of the funds can be found in appendix 4). These funds specify that each investment by the fund must conform to certain ethical criteria in addition to satisfying certain investment objectives. In this way, investors in these funds can be satisfied that the stocks or other investments of the fund do not violate publicly stated ethical standards.

The funds have different ethical criteria, which means that potential investors should examine these criteria closely to determine whether they match their own social and political concerns. These funds are suited for RRSP-holders who want to establish general ethical criteria for their investments, and employ professional management of their plans at the same time.

For more information on ethical mutual funds, see the next chapter on investments.

Stocks and Other Securities

Stocks and other securities may be the most difficult and risky form of investing for ethical and conventional investors. In order to invest your RRSP in securities you will need to open a self-directed RRSP, which is discussed later in this chapter.

Stocks require a fair amount of time and a fair knowledge of the financial pitfalls of the market, and they are suited only to those ethical investors who have thought extensively about their ethical standards. However, for the sophisticated ethical RRSP-holder an investment in stocks can be extremely rewarding. An investment in a particular company gives you the satisfaction of knowing that you are investing according to a carefully defined set of social and political criteria.

You can also invest RRSP money in other corporate securities such as bonds and debentures. For more information on these, see the next chapter on investments.

Special Investments

This is a grab-bag of RRSP products, and each one carries its own special financial and ethical considerations.

First, some ethical investors may want to use RRSP money to purchase shares in a cooperative enterprise or credit union. You may be a member of the cooperative or credit union, or you may purchase a preferred share offered by the enterprise. A preferred share will offer a dividend, but it does not give you any equity in the enterprise. This kind of investment, however, allows you to assist the cooperative movement in Canada through your RRSP savings. It is considered a risky way of investing RRSP money and you will need a self-directed RRSP to purchase such shares. You should also be careful to ensure that the shares do qualify under the RRSP rules.

It is not easy to find a cooperative needing this kind of financing, but one of the cooperative consulting organizations listed in appendix 3 (under alternative investments) may be able to help.

Second, you may be interested in using RRSP money to buy shares in a private company that survives your special ethical screens. This is also considered quite risky, and there are complex rules governing what companies are eligible. You should consult a lawyer if you are planning such an investment.

Many investors may want to consider purchasing a mortgage — perhaps even on their own home — for their RRSP (more on this under self-directed RRSPs).

Finally, insurance companies also offer a variety of annuities or life-insurance contracts registered as RRSPs. Many financial planners advise clients not to purchase this kind of RRSP, however, because returns on some types of these contracts are not as favourable as other RRSP investments. Be sure to get full information on the returns that such a plan would earn.

SELF-DIRECTED *VERSUS* ADMINISTERED RRSPs

Trust companies and securities dealers, along with a few banks, have been promoting self-directed RRSPs during the last few years. Self-directed RRSPs have some economic as well as ethical advantages. But they require a fair-sized portfolio, in addition to a fair amount of management time and market expertise. Clearly, they are best for experienced investors.

A self-directed RRSP differs from an administered RRSP in that the plan-holder decides what investments to place in his or her plan. This gives the plan-holder the flexibility to purchase low-priced stocks, for example, or move out of bonds whose value may be declining as inflation rises. Mutual funds can also be purchased through self-directed RRSPs.

Self-directed plans work much like bank accounts. When you start a self-directed RRSP, you open a plan in which you can buy, sell or transfer investments. You are personally responsible for ensuring that your annual contributions do not exceed federal limits and that any investment qualifies under federal regulations. To buy, sell or transfer investments, you must contact the institution acting for you, which maintains a trading team to execute transactions. Annual fees for self-directed RRSPs are usually $100. Additional commissions are charged for stock trades, purchases of mutual funds with commissions and some other investment transactions.

The economic advantages of a self-directed RRSP lie in the flexibility to buy, sell or transfer investments under optimum conditions. It allows you to change your investment mix when stock prices rise or fall, interest rates rise or fall, or when mutual-fund values change. In a period of volatile markets, this can add appreciably to the performance of your portfolio.

One unique aspect of self-directed plans that may be of interest to some investors is the ability to lend *yourself* funds secured by a mortgage on your own home. The mortgage can cover all or part of the value of your home. It must be a first or second mortgage on a residential property in Canada, and it must be government-insured and administered by a National Housing Act approved lender. You must pay interest equal to prevailing market rates and you must meet National Housing Act lending requirements. The funds can be used to make investments, to provide emergency cash if you lose your job, or for any other purpose. The annual cost is usually $100 or $150 in addition to the self-directed RRSP fee. There may also be appraisal and legal fees at the time the mortgage is set up.

Because of the $100 annual fee, financial counsellors usually recommend self-directed RRSPs for investors with an RRSP portfolio of at least $10,000, as previously mentioned. You have to ensure that the gains made in a self-directed plan are sufficiently better than gains in an administered plan to justify the extra $100 fee. Counsellors also recommend that self-directed plans are best for experienced investors, who can make best use of flexible investment options and avoid the pitfalls of bad investments.

Ethical Considerations of Self-Directed RRSPs
Self-directed RRSPs carry some benefits for investors interested in the ethical consequences of their investments. As mentioned earlier, investors interested in particular companies because of their ethical history can invest their RRSP money directly in those companies by using a self-directed plan. In so doing, you can make your investments conform exactly to your ethical criteria (labour practices, clean technology and so on). By relying on an ethical mutual fund, you must accept the criteria set down by the fund managers and, consequently, may have to accept some criteria that you do not enthusiastically support.

Self-directed RRSPs also give added flexibility to aggressive ethical investors who are interested in specialized investments.

One last point about self-directed RRSPs is of interest to many ethical investors. The only province in which *credit unions* are authorized to offer self-directed RRSPs is British Columbia. However, in early 1987, credit-union officials began discussions with federal Department of Finance officials to change the regulations to enable credit unions to offer self-directed RRSPs. At the time of writing (1987), the credit union officials had received a sympathetic hearing, but federal officials had pointed out that amendments were needed to provincial legislation.

WHAT HAPPENS WHEN YOU RETIRE?

Under federal regulations, you must collapse your RRSP by December 31 in the year in which you turn seventy-one. If you are nearing this date and age, you should be considering your alternatives because there are very different ways of managing your money after your plan is collapsed. The alternatives carry both economic and ethical consequences.

Basically, your alternatives for managing your post-RRSP money fall into four categories: 1) you can collapse your plan, withdraw the money and pay tax on the proceeds; 2) you can transfer the RRSP fund into a Registered Retirement Income Fund (RRIF); 3) you can buy an annuity with your RRSP funds; 4) you can carry out a combination of these options.

Collapsing your plan can have serious tax consequences if you do it in a single lump sum. You will have to pay tax at your marginal rate of taxation which, if your fund is a typical size, will be about 50 per cent in most provinces. This means that half of your fund will go to Revenue Canada. It is possible to withdraw certain amounts from your RRSP gradually up to the time you are seventy-one. This may have advantages if you want cash at certain times and yet still want the remainder of the RRSP to continue to earn income tax-free.

The second alternative is to purchase an RRIF. An RRIF works much like an RRSP and is offered by credit unions, banks, trust companies, insurance companies and some mutual-fund dealers and stock brokers. You can purchase RRIF investments, or you can have a self-administered RRIF.

This is how an RRIF works. Once you transfer your RRSP money into an RRIF, you must withdraw a minimum each year that is calculated according to the difference between your current age and age ninety. This formula provides for increasing minimum payments as you get older until the fund is exhausted in your nintieth year. That way you cannot keep deferring tax payments indefinitely. For example, if you begin an RRIF when you turn seventy, the first year you must withdraw at least 1/20 of the fund. In the second, you withdraw 1/19. In the third, you withdraw 1/18, and so on.

RRIFs were first allowed by law in 1978, but they have only recently become popular with federal budget changes in 1986. The most important change introduced by the budget revisions permitted RRIF holders to withdraw as much as they want from their plan at any time, so long as they withdraw at least the annual minimum. Previously, RRIF holders could withdraw no more than the fractional amount, which provided an income considered too low by most retirees, particularly in the first years of retirement. Now, however, RRIF holders can "customize" their pensions.

RRIFs require some management. You have the option of placing part of your RRIF in growth investments or staying with interest- bearing vehicles. Some financial advisers recommend a number of different types of interest-bearing investments or bonds. This way, the fund is secure, while it can take advantage of changes in interest rates.

RRIFs differ from annuities in that, with an annuity, your RRSP lump sum is turned over to an institution holding your annuity and you receive a predetermined income. There are different kinds of annuities, but the amount of your annuity income will vary with current interest rates, age, life expectancy and provisions for your estate. Annuities are generally offered by insurance companies.

Annuities come with fixed or variable income and offer a number of different options. A life annuity provides regular payments for as long as you live. When you die, there is no money turned over to your spouse or estate. The insurance company gets the rest of your fund. This differs from a joint-and-last-survivor annuity, which will continue payments to your spouse for as long as he or she lives. You also have the choice of specifying a minimum payment guarantee. This guarantee ensures that your spouse or estate receives payments for a number of years even if you die before the guarantee expires. Generally payments are lower with a joint than with single annuity, because the insurance company will likely have to make a payout for a longer period of time.

From an ethical point of view, the biggest difference between RRIFs and annuities is that, with an RRIF, the investor makes the ethical choices about where his or her money will be invested. You have the choice of investing with an institution that you feel ethically comfortable with, and you also have the choice to specify certain investments. Your ethical choice of investments may become constrained as you get older, because you will likely want to shy away from stocks, bonds or growth funds. With an annuity, however, you lose all choice over the ethical determination of your funds. In addition, if you choose a life annuity, the only institution you will be able to deal with is an insurance company.

Investors in most provinces who appreciate the value of credit unions, and who want to stick with credit unions for their post-RRSP products, have no choice. They must take out an RRIF. Credit unions welcomed the 1986 budget changes because members who had been saving money in a credit-union RRSP often switched to a life-insurance company for an annuity when the RRSP matured. Now, more credit union members have an opportunity to keep their money with their institiution. In its 1986 annual report, Vancouver City Savings Credit Union, for example, stated that a large percentage of maturing RRSPs that had previously been converted to life annuities had remained with VanCity as RRIF contracts. A growing number of credit unions are offering RRIFs following the 1986 budget changes.

Since you have the option of making use of a combination of cash-ins, RRIFs and annuities, it makes sense to review all the alternatives in order to "customize" a pension that is suited for your age, health, marital and family status, and any expected changes in your future income.

A FINAL WORD ABOUT RRSP ETHICAL CHOICES

There are three things to think about when you consider the ethical choices involved in purchasing a retirement savings product.

You first have to decide which institution you want to deal with. This choice becomes more complex in big cities because of the large numbers of banks, trust companies, securities dealers, insurance companies and credit unions from which to choose. Second you also have to decide which type of retirement-savings product is best for you. For RRSPs, this means choosing between administered and self-directed plans. For post-RRSP products, this means choosing between RRIFs and annuities or putting your money in a combination of the two. Third and finally, you have to decide which investment best meets your ethical criteria.

For people who want to invest in guaranteed RRSPs, credit unions offer a clear ethical alternative to the banks and trust companies. For people who want growth potential but do not have the resources to manage their investments, an ethical mutual fund is best. For those interested in stocks, bonds, debentures or other specialized investments, a self-directed RRSP or RRIF is required.

3

INVESTING — PUTTING AWAY FOR GAIN AND GOOD

As the ethical investment movement grows in maturity, activists within the movement are pointing to a distinction in the kinds of investments that are defined as "ethical."

On the one hand, there are investments in mutual funds, stocks and other corporate investments that are screened to fulfill certain social criteria. They are what most people in the business community have come to know as ethical, socially responsible or screened investments. They are the investments that have captured the imagination of most of the investing public since they hold the possibility of combining traditional investments with a progressive world view.

However, other people involved in the application of social values to investment are not as concerned with ethical criteria as they are with serving local communities and providing jobs for the unemployed. This field of ethical investment is, as noted before, coming to be known as "alternative investment." Alternative investment is intimately related to the growing field of community economic development, a process that gives ordinary people in a community greater say over their economic institutions. Community economic development activists believe that the best way to preserve jobs is to unleash the entrepreneurial capabilities of ordinary people by placing economic institutions under democratic control.

A consultant's report prepared in 1986 for the Canadian Alternative Investment Co-operative, an investment fund for religious and charitable organizations, put it this way:

> While socially responsible investment is concerned with the "good," the participation of the investor is essentially passive and the principal consideration is achieving a "nice" return. In contrast, alternative investment is more broadly

focused than simply a "clean" return on investment and has a more active interest in the outcome.

While alternative investing may ultimately hold more potential than ethical investing for progressive social change, opportunities for investors are more difficult to find and use. Investors interested in alternative investment opportunities should be prepared to do some digging, and may have to accept a higher level of risk.

ETHICAL INVESTMENT CRITERIA

If you choose the ethical-investing route, the first thing you have to do is decide what ethical criteria you want to apply to your investments. This does not mean that you have to arrive at an exhaustive list of your social values, but it does mean that you should think about what social concerns really matter to you.

To begin with, you might want to think about what priority you give to the issue of South African investment. No single issue has galvanized the ethical investment movement more than South African apartheid. Several ethical-investment funds contain screens against companies operating in countries that practice racial inequality. The Crown Life Commitment Fund, for example, a Canadian ethical fund for pension investments, specifically avoids investments in companies doing business with South Africa.

While concerns over apartheid have dominated the ethical-investment movement, they are gradually falling to the wayside as fewer and fewer companies retain South African affiliates or subsidiaries. According to figures compiled by the Taskforce on the Churches and Corporate Responsibility and federal representatives overseeing Canadian corporate conduct in South Africa, there were thirteen companies with affiliates or investments in South Africa or Namibia, which is under illegal occupation by South Africa, in April 1987. Of these thirteen, three have subsequently indicated they intend to pull out. Because there are so few Canadian companies with investments in South Africa, the battle against apartheid is losing its urgency as a concern for Canadian ethical investors — though the war itself is not over yet.

Table 5

Canadian Companies with Affiliates in South Africa, April 1987	
Companies	*No. of affiliates*
AMCA International Ltd.[1]	1
Bauer and Crosby Inc.	1
Bayer Foreign Investments Ltd. (No report for 1986)	5
Champion Road Machinery Marketing Ltd.	1
Cobra Metals and Minerals Inc.[2] (No report for 1986)	2
Ford Motor Co. of Canada Ltd.[3]	1
JKS Boyles International Inc.	1
Menora Resources Inc.	1
National Business Systems Inc. (No report for 1986)	1
QIT - Fer et Titane Inc.	1
Sternson Ltd.	1
Varity Corp. (formerly Massey-Ferguson)	2

Canadian Companies with Investments in Namibia,[4] April 1987

Rio Algom Ltd.
Menora Resources Inc.
(Status uncertain as it has not responded to a letter of inquiry)

Source: Taskforce on the Churches and Corporate Responsibility, Derived from the *Canadian Code of Conduct—Canadian Companies in South Africa*, June 1987 report
[1]AMCA has announced its intention to dispose of its South African affiliate, BOMAG.
[2]Cobra has announced its intention of dissociating itself from its South African interests.
[3]On June 15, 1987, Ford announced that it is discussing divestment.
[4]Namibia is under illegal occupation by South Africa.

Other criteria are coming to dominate discussion of social screens. This discussion is reaching a high level of sophistication as a result of work by the major churches.

The Committee on Social Responsibility in Investment Policy of the Presbyterian Church in Canada has a set of ethical guidelines developed in consultation with the Canadian Conference of Catholic Bishops. The guidelines set out questions that may be raised about the social responsibility of companies doing business in Canada or other countries. The full set of guidelines has been reproduced in appendix 2, but here is a short outline:

- The rights and needs of employees. Adequate and competitive wages, safeguards for health, safety and job security, recognition of trade-union rights, employee participation in the management process.
- The economic development of the community or country in which companies operate. Impact of operations in the community, job creation, capital reinvestment.
- Social and environmental conditions. Inordinate control over local economies or land, requirements that the workforce migrate from home in order to get a job, jobs for minority groups, pollution.
- Civil, political and religious liberties. Operations in countries with repressive régimes, operations in countries that practise apartheid or impose restrictions on religious freedom.
- Production and marketing of products. Luxury goods or basic needs, harmful products, arms production, truthful advertising practices, monopoly control of markets.

As you can see, these guidelines are simply questions that ethical investors can ask of companies in which they are considering an investment. They do not pose minimum performance criteria, and leave it up to the *investor* to decide whether particular companies measure up.

Tim Smith, executive director of the New York-based Interfaith Centre on Corporate Responsibility, goes one step further. He not only offers a set of guidelines for ethical investors but suggests certain minimum standards that companies should meet to qualify for ethical investment. Here are Smith's criteria, as outlined in Toronto in May 1986 during a workshop on socially responsible investment.

- No investment in South Africa, or other repressive régimes.

- No investment in Nestlé's or other companies, such as some pharmaceutical companies, with unjust marketing practices.
- Equal ethnic and sexual employment opportunities.
- Businesses controlled by minorities should be given preference in supply purchases.
- No nuclear weapons production, nor production for the Strategic Defence Initiative (Star Wars).
- Compliance with health and safety standards.
- Responsible environmental protection and toxic waste management.
- Employment of energy-conservation techniques and non-nuclear energy.
- A fair international debt record.

Some ethical investors may be single-issue investors, concerned with a narrow set of social screens. Others may have a broad world view encompassing wide concerns about the quality of the environment, international social justice, employment practices and corporate conduct. By using these investment guidelines, you can get a better flavour of the social concerns of the ethical investment movement. In turn, these guidelines can help you sort out your own personal ethical criteria.

Once you decide what ethical screens to apply, there are two kinds of investments open to you: mutual funds or direct corporate investments, such as stocks or bonds.

ETHICAL MUTUAL FUNDS

Ethical mutual funds in Canada are tiny compared with some of the giant conventional funds which have grown enormously during the last few years. The largest fund employing social criteria in investments, the Quebec Federation of Labour Solidarity Fund, had assets of nearly $100 million by March 1987. But it was dwarfed by the largest of the conventional equity funds, Industrial Growth, which stood at about $1.5 billion.

Still, members of the Canadian Network for Ethical Investment, an association of brokers, investment advisors, investors and interested individuals, say that the movement is growing fast and holds large potential. Larry Trunkey, founder of the network and an investment consultant with Galatea Consulting Ltd. in Victoria, British Columbia, estimates that about 10 per cent of the $150-billion-worth of Canadian pension money could eventually be controlled by the ethical investment movement.

Ethical mutual funds operate, in part, like conventional mutual funds, which entrust investors' money to professional managers. In return for cash, the investor receives a certain number of "units," or shares, in the fund. The fund managers then invest that cash in stocks and other investments, which earn a return for the fund-holders. The value of the units is determined on a daily or weekly basis.

Fund managers use professional expertise and judgment to buy and sell investments and alter the portfolio mix to suit changing conditions. They also pool investments so that a loss in any one stock does not seriously damage the overall return to the fund. A sponsoring organization may want to establish a fund for a particular clientele, but the sponsor usually does not manage the fund. In these cases, the sponsor hires a professional financial manager to look after the operation of the fund while it reserves the right to set the overall investment policies.

One important thing to keep in mind about mutual funds is that they are *not* guaranteed investments like bank accounts, GICs or Canada Savings Bonds. Returns from mutual funds fluctuate with the stock market, rising and falling. If you require a high degree of liquidity (an easily accessible source of cash) you should avoid mutual funds.

With an ethical mutual fund, fund managers or sponsors not only choose investments on a financial basis, such as long-term growth, income or minimal risk, but also screen out certain investments that do not meet the ethical criteria established by the sponsor.

Ethical Surveillance of Mutual Funds
Ethical mutual funds are expected to drop a company from their portfolio if the manager or sponsor receives information that a company is contravening the ethical guidelines. The Ethical Growth Fund of Vancouver City Savings Credit Union, for example, dropped Atco Industries Ltd. when it signed a contract to produce military tank equipment. The Fund also dropped Moore Corp. after it learned that that Moore, a business-forms manufacturer, maintained some employees in South Africa. (Moore has subsequently pulled out of South Africa.)

The managers and sponsors of ethical funds have a certain leeway in interpreting the guidelines. For instance, an exemption might apply to a holding company which has an interest in a company with a subsidiary in South Africa. Or it might also apply to a company that normally produces non-military goods but receives a short-term contract for military production. Bob Quart, manager of trust services for Van-

City, puts it this way: "It's not a perfect science. Everything is in degrees, but we try to achieve precisely what we represent ourselves to be without being a protest group.... There are going to be some very difficult calls, and when a call is really difficult, when there's a lot of gray shaded areas, we tend to give them the benefit of the doubt."

Moira Hutchinson, coordinator of the Taskforce on the Churches and Corporate Responsibility, offers this word of advice: "One of the things that consumers are going to have to be concerned about, I think, is that they can't assume that by putting their money into a mutual fund that their criteria are really being met." She recalls this word of warning from Tim Smith of the ICCR in New York: "Among the large number of American mutual funds that apply social screens, there are a couple that you could drive a nuclear submarine through."

Investors who do place money with ethical funds are advised to become familiar with the companies in the portfolio of their fund, and to watch for the names of those companies in the news media. It is also advisable to purchase products or services from these companies to get some personal familiarity with how they operate. If one of those companies does something you do not like, you are advised to write to the fund manager or sponsor to complain.

Nevertheless, for investors concerned with the social consequences of their financial decisions, an ethical fund is better than a conventional fund. An ethical fund gives the investor some assurance that certain ethical criteria are being met. The managers of a conventional mutual fund may or may not follow ethical criteria, but the fundholders have no knowledge of what, if any, ethical criteria are being applied.

Financial Performance of Ethical Funds

In terms of return, conventional investment theory states that ethical funds will probably not perform as well as funds that do not apply social screens. As the argument goes, social screens limit the number of companies available for investment and thus reduce the opportunities for gain.

While this makes sense in theory, the practical limitations on ethical funds are often quite small. For example, the Ethical Growth Fund reviewed all of the 300 companies contained in the main Toronto Stock Exchange index before the fund started operating in 1986. Of these 300, 45 were eliminated because they did not fit into the VanCity ethical criteria. That left more than 83 per cent of the stock market's 300 largest companies available for investment.

However, with more specialized ethical funds there may be a greater narrowing of choices. In the United States, the New Alternatives Fund invests solely in solar and alternative-energy companies. But because New Alternatives has invested in promising technologies, its track record has been fairly good. In 1986, the fund's value increased by 22.7 per cent, which placed it 123rd out of 1,100 funds.

"You don't have to sacrifice financial return by investing in harmony with your conscience," says Larry Trunkey. "That doesn't mean that you're going to have the top performance, but you are going to have a respectable performance."

In a review of the performance of the U.S. ethical funds, Babson-United Investment Advisors Inc. of Boston put it less positively. In the March 17, 1987 issue of the *United Mutual Fund Selector*, Babson-United concluded: "Returns on these funds have not been impressive, generally hovering somewhat below leading market indicators. However, if you feel that investing in companies which support social welfare is as important as profit margins, then ethical mutual funds might be worth considering."

Canadian ethical funds have not been operating for very long, so long-term appraisals are impossible. However, detailed financial comparisons of recent returns are provided in appendix 4. Ethical Growth earned a return of 9 per cent in the year up to June 30, 1987, and In-

Table 6

How U.S. Ethical Funds Have Fared: Percentage Change in Asset Value

Fund	2 mos.	1 yr.	3 yrs.
Calvert Social Managed Growth	10.3	20.5	50.1
Dreyfus Third Century	13.8	9.7	33.8
New Alternatives	15.3	28.2	49.0
Parnassus Fund	31.3	24.8	49.0
Pax World Fund	10.2	14.0	38.4
Pioneer Bond Fund	1.5	9.1	46.2
Pioneer Fund	16.0	18.2	36.5
Pioneer II	14.2	19.0	40.8
Pioneer Three	18.0	19.5	43.3
Standard and Poors 500 stocks	17.9	28.9	64.4

Source: *United Mutual Fund Selector*, March 17, 1987: Babson-United Investment Advisors Inc., Boston, Mass.

vestors Summa Fund earned 5.2 per cent in the six months ending on the same date. The QFL Solidarity Fund, which determines a new value of its shares twice a year, earned 8.9 per cent in the year ending October 31, 1986. By comparison, the Toronto Stock Exchange 300 index — a measure of prices of the top 300 share issues on the TSE — rose 22 per cent in the first six months of 1987.

Comparisons of new funds with long-standing conventional funds and market measures, such as the TSE 300, are somewhat misleading. New funds, whether ethical or conventional, have a high proportion of the deposits contributed by unit-holders in cash, rather than investments in the stock market or elsewhere. This is because fund managers cannot place cash in the market as soon as they receive it. They must save it until an opportunity arises to purchase attractive shares. As a result, a large proportion of unit-holders' money is earning less than optimum returns.

To help you determine whether a fund is performing acceptably, here are a few guides. First, compare the performance of the fund against interest rates for investment certificates and Canada Savings Bonds. Because you are accepting a higher level of risk with mutual funds, you should also receive a higher return. Second, compare your mutual fund performance against the TSE 300 and the Standard and Poor's 500 Index, the broadest measure of stock activity in the United States. Mutual funds should perform better than the market as a whole. Third and finally, you can compare the performance of your fund against the average performance of conventional funds of a similar type. Funds are categorized as equity funds, which hold stock market shares; money market funds, which hold bonds, debentures and preferred shares; and balanced funds, which hold both types of investments.

Daily newspapers carry listings of the unit values of funds. Other sources of information on mutual funds are contained in chapter 7.

Making the Decision to Invest in a Mutual Fund

In order to decide whether an ethical mutual fund is better than another type of ethical investment, you should ask a number of questions about yourself. These questions pertain both to your financial situation (see chapter 2 for a discussion of the financial aspects of RRSP investing) and the amount of time, energy and resources you wish to spend on financial management.

From a financial point of view, are you willing to accept the level of risk posed by mutual funds? Unlike GICs, terms deposits, bank accounts, Canada Savings Bonds and treasury bills, mutual funds are not guaranteed by governments or deposit-insurance organizations. Because of this risk, many mutual-fund advisers recommend that funds be held for at least four years, and perhaps as long as ten or fifteen years, to take advantage of rising and falling stock-market cycles. To help you assess the risk of particular funds, the financial press publishes measures of mutual-fund variability. These measures are discussed in chapter 7.

Different types of funds have different levels of risk. The ethical mutual funds are generally equity funds, which do not carry as high a risk as conventional speculative funds, but they are higher-risk than mortgage or money-market funds.

Another financial consideration is your age. Just as you have to take account of your age in retirement planning, you must take account of it in investment planning: you must decide whether you are young enough to risk placing retirement assets in a variable investment. If you need assets in a few years for retirement income, you may want to stick with guaranteed investments.

Again, are you willing to pay a commission to purchase units in the fund? Not all ethical mutual funds charge a commission, but many impose a "front-end load" to acquire units. Front-end loads range between 0 and 8.5 per cent on Canadian ethical mutual funds. This means that, if you purchase $10,000 worth of units in a fund with a front-end load of 5 per cent, you will actually receive only $9,500 worth of units. The additional $500 goes to the sales representatives, and to cover other operating costs.

Finally, does an investment in mutual funds fit in with your RRSP and tax strategies? (See chapters 2 and 4.) If you make the decision to invest in a mutual fund, you must decide whether to use unregistered funds for the investment, or whether you want the mutual fund as part of your RRSP or RRIF. Canadian mutual funds generally qualify for the advantageous dividend tax credit and capital-gains exemption. This means that you may want to place unregistered money in a mutual fund, and keep your RRSP or RRIF money for guaranteed investments.

U.S. Funds

The funds so far discussed are Canadian ethical funds. They are based in Canada and are permitted by provincial securities commissions to solicit investments in certain provinces in Canada. But Canadian investors also have the opportunity to place money with ethical funds in the United States or other countries. U.S. funds may appeal to certain

Canadian investors who prefer the ethical criteria of, or the returns on, U.S. funds. However, there are a few things — from a financial point of view — to keep in mind if you are considering an investment in a U.S. mutual fund.

First, there are restrictions on using RRSP or RRIF money in non-Canadian investments. Remember that at least 90 per cent of a particular portfolio registered as an RRSP or RRIF must be invested in Canadian securities or other Canadian investments.

Second, while Canadian equity mutual funds generally qualify for the Canadian dividend tax credit, dividends earned in U.S. mutual funds will not qualify. Ordinarily, with dividends received from Canadian corporations, you can claim the credit, if the shares are held outside an RRSP. The credit applies only to dividends on taxable Canadian corporations. Because U.S. companies do not pay Canadian taxes, the credit does not apply.

Third, you should consider the financial impact on your investment of changes in the relative value of the Canadian and U.S. dollars. If you expect the Canadian dollar to fall and the U.S. dollar to rise, a U.S. investment might become more attractive. If the opposite is true, a U.S. investment becomes less attractive. During 1987, the Canadian dollar was relatively stable against its U.S. counterpart, so currency considerations did not play as large a role in investment decisions as they had in the past.

Profiles and addresses for the American ethical funds are contained in appendix 6.

Pension, Church, Charity, Union and Other Group Investments
While the funds discussed so far are available to individual investors, there are other ethical funds operating in Canada that are available only to groups. The sponsors and managers of these funds — known as institutional ethical funds — have decided to cater to organizations for philosophical or business reasons, to keep their costs down or to avoid the reporting requirements imposed by securities legislation on funds offering sales to individuals.

While it may not be possible to invest in these funds as an individual, it may be possible to persuade the directors of your company pension plan, your church fund, your union or any other group to which you belong to place money with one of them. If you are a member of a registered pension plan negotiated through a collective agreement, you may want to ask the union representatives on the pension committee if they favour switching the pension fund to an ethical investment fund. Unions are becoming increasingly sensitive to the fact that they share responsibility for the collective management of billions of pension dollars annually. These funds should be placed in investments that are consistent with the basic principles of the union movement. Similarly, charities or church groups with large endowments are becoming more and more sensitive to the need to invest those funds in socially responsible investments.

Even if you are not a member of a registered pension plan, it may be possible to have your employer establish a group RRSP on the behalf of the employees. Most of the ethical funds available to individual investors will also accept group RRSPs; but one of the funds available only to groups — the Crown Commitment Fund — is set up specifically to manage pensions and group RRSPs. A group RRSP can be organized under a payroll deduction program and can offer employees the option of contributing to an ethical fund as well as a conventional fund. Group RRSPs have become increasingly popular in recent years and are now offered by many unions and professsional associations as well as employers. One of the advantages of investing in group RRSPs is that you may be able build up a sizeable group contribution that can provide savings in front-end loads that would not be available to you as an individual investor.

Profiles and addresses for these institutional ethical funds are contained in appendix 7.

STOCKS AND OTHER SECURITIES

For novices, the stock market can be an intimidating place. It has its own language, which is carefully cultivated by investment professionals to protect their position as "insiders." There is also the peculiar behaviour of floor traders, who shout at each other to execute buy and sell orders. This gives the exchange an aura of a cattle auction, rather than a rational place of business.

But for ethical investors stock-market investments can be a rewarding place to put money. They allow you to choose companies that perfectly match your ethical criteria. They can also give you a say — although usually only a tiny say — in the operations of the company in which you invest.

The stock markets are becoming increasingly attractive to Canadians. A survey conducted for the Toronto Stock Exchange in 1986 showed that about 3.2 million Canadians — 18 per cent of the adult population — owned shares in publicly traded stocks or equity mutual funds. This was up from 11 per cent in 1983. About 2.8 million of these people held stock directly, while about a million held equity mutual funds.

Rising share prices were responsible for this increase. However, many experts said that stock prices, which began a five-year run-up in 1982, were long overdue for a slump when the massive crash occurred in the fall of 1987. The outlook for 1988 is uncertain.

If you choose to purchase stocks or other securities, the first thing you must do is research a short list of companies that are appealing for ethical and financial reasons. Once you settle on the companies in which you want to invest, you can then choose the type of security — stock, bond, debenture etc. — that fits into your financial requirements. This section sets out the broad outlines of ethical stock market investing. Chapter 7 on resources discusses how to research and purchase stocks.

What Are Stocks?

Stocks are shares in a company that are traded in one of two ways: 1) they can be bought and sold in public markets (stock exchanges); 2) they can be traded privately by investment dealers through the so-called over-the-counter (OTC) market. The OTC market is much smaller than the exchange markets, and government securities commissions place more stringent requirements on companies issuing stock on the exchanges. In Canada, the exchanges are: the Toronto Stock Exchange, the Montreal Exchange, the Vancouver Stock Exchange and the Alberta Exchange.

There are two basic kinds of stocks, and stocks are distinguished from other securities such as bonds, debentures and options. The kinds of stocks are: common shares, which carry rights to vote on company matters; and preferred shares, which usually do not carry voting rights. Preferred shares are given this name because they rank ahead of common stock in the payout of dividends (profits distributed to the shareholders) and in the distribution of assets if the company is liquidated. Preferred shares usually carry a set dividend that is payable to the shareholder at the discretion of the board of directors of the company.

Since the board of directors is obliged to pay the dividend on preferred shares before a common-stock dividend is declared, preferred shares are a better bet for people more interested in income than capital appreciation. Common stock is usually more volatile in price, and holds better potential for capital growth (and loss). Common stock also generally trades at a higher price relative to preferred shares. This is because companies wishing to take over another company will have to make an offer to purchase the common stock, not the preferred shares. Thus, buyers of common shares are paying for the possibility that someone in the future may wish to pay them an even higher price for their shares in order to purchase control of the company.

Still, preferred shares are attractive to many investors because they are generally more secure and offer set dividends. Sometimes preferred shares come with voting rights at some future time.

From an ethical point of view, however, there is a debate about whether preferred shares are an appropriate investment. One of the essential premises of the ethical investment movement is that investors have a right to voice concern over the way their investment money is being used. Preferred shareholders have no greater say over the operations of their company than depositors have over the business of a bank. Thus, if your company takes an action of which you disapprove, your only option is to sell your shares. This is an ineffective means of protest because you are unable to confront the senior management or board of directors of the company directly.

The other side of the debate goes like this. If you are reasonably comfortable, from an ethical point of view, with the company you have chosen, it may not be necessary to worry about whether you will ever have to confront senior management. This is an important consideration when you remember that shareholders have little real say over the companies in which they invest. Only rarely have church-sponsored resolutions on South African divestment attracted more than 5-per-cent support at shareholder meetings. Most big companies in Canada are controlled by institutions, and these institutions side with management against any boat-rocking shareholder action.

The other types of securities also carry ethical implications. Corporate bonds are similar to Canada Savings Bonds, except that they are issued by private companies. Bonds are debt obligations that are secured by specific assets of the company should the company fold. Debentures are similar, except that they are not secured by specific assets.

From an ethical point of view, bonds and debentures are similar to preferred shares. There is no voting right connected with them, but if they are purchased in companies previously subjected to social screens, they make acceptable ethical investments.

However, in Canada, there is a particular problem concerning bonds and debentures that is of concern to many investors. This concerns the sale of bonds and debentures by provincial electric utility commissions. These utilities, of which Ontario Hydro and Hydro Québec are the largest, do an enormous amount of borrowing through bonds and debentures sold through stock-brokerage firms. For example, Hydro Québec issued $325 million in new debentures in July 1987 — $120 million maturing in 1997 at 9.75 per cent, and $205 million maturing in 2012 at 10.25 per cent.

Many ethical investors disapprove of such bonds because of concerns about the environmental records of the utilities. For instance, environmentalists and native peoples were angered by the James Bay hydro project. Similarly, the Ethical Growth Fund of the Vancouver City Savings Credit Union will not invest in Ontario Hydro bonds because of its "screen" against companies involved with the nuclear industry. Ontario Hydro generates a large proportion of its electricity from nuclear plants.

Because of these special ethical problems, socially conscious investors should consider whether they want to purchase bonds offered by electric utilities. Bonds offered by municipalities, which use them to pay for roads, sewers and other local services, may be a more acceptable ethical alternative.

Options of interest only to extremely sophisticated investors are contracts between a buyer and seller that give the buyer the right to purchase a stock or bond from the seller at a specified price for a particular length of time. These are used mainly to reduce the risk of market fluctuations, but they have other advantages. While few ethical investors have the high level of knowledge needed to trade in options, options can be part of an ethical portfolio as long as the underlying securities have been previously screened.

Do You Want to be in the Market?
As mentioned previously in this chapter, there has been a dramatic increase in the number of Canadian investors involved with the stock markets. These people represent a minority of Canadian investors, but their number is growing. How do you know whether you should be among them?

First, keep in mind that you need enough income or assets to be able to lose money on the market. Some ethical companies are considered among the best blue-chip stocks available. But there are fluctuations in the market, and you should be prepared to lose money. As a rule of thumb, Marathon Brown, a discount stock-brokerage firm, requires its customers to have an account of no less than $5,000. The company says that this amount ensures that the customer has enough cash to take the risks inherent in the stock market. If you are using RRSP money, financial planners recommend that you hold an RRSP of at least $10,000 before you consider trading in stock.

From an ethical point of view, you will want to ask whether you prefer the stock markets to other types of ethical investments. As previously mentioned, companies can be subjected to ethical screens before you invest in their shares. But you might believe that there are preferable ways of investing your money than in major corporations which have little difficulty raising capital. You may think that it is more important to help finance local enterprises or your community credit union.

From a financial point of view, you should review the same questions posed about mutual funds in the earlier section. But you should understand that investments directly in the market pose a greater risk than investments in mutual funds, which are managed by investment professionals.

The stock markets are dominated by large institutional — often international — investors. Many observers, for example, attributed much of the 1987 bull market to Japanese interest in North American stock markets created by changes in the relative value of the U.S. dollar and Japanese yen. In order to be comfortable with your stock-market investment, you should have at least a rudimentary understanding of fundamental economic conditions in Canada and abroad.

In addition, you will want to become familiar with some of the technical factors that motivate the stock market. For example, one of the things you should examine before buying any stock is its price earnings (P/E) ratio, the price of a share divided by its earnings per share for the latest twelve-month period. If a stock is trading at $40 a share, and it generates earnings of $2 a share, the P/E ratio is 20:1 — generally considered too high to be profitable. This could mean that the stock is overbought and will eventually head downward.

Chapter 7 gives some tips on stock-market research.

Investment Clubs
If you have a group of friends, relatives or acquaintances who are interested in the ethical-investment movement, it may be possible to rally these people to form an ethical-investment club.

Some clubs start with an initial investment of as little as $50 or $100, and then require monthly installments of $25 or $50. The money is invested according to ethical and financial criteria established by the group, and monitored by the group. Conducting trades through a discount brokerage firm keeps costs down. The club should establish a written set of bylaws, and operating procedures should be thoroughly discussed by everyone involved. The stickiest point of contention for most clubs is how to redeem shares in the club when members want to quit.

Information on how to establish an investment club can be obtained from the Canadian Association of Investment Clubs (address in appendix 3).

Shareholder Activism

Most ethical investors will want to avoid companies that contravene their ethical criteria. In special cases, however, you may want to place funds in shares of companies that have mixed ethical records. This may seem like an odd proposition at first glance, but there are occasions when a shareholder may want to deliberately purchase shares in a company to give him or her a say over the operations of that company. Take the divestment issue, for example. Most ethical investors take a straight "No South African investment" position. Other ethical investors believe that withdrawal might actually worsen conditions for black employees. In this case, an investor may want to purchase shares in a company operating in South Africa, but will want the company to operate with the highest employment standards.

This can also happen with shareholders who are satisfied with their companies on most issues, but are troubled by one or two ethical concerns.

The Taskforce on the Churches and Corporate Responsibility and Greenpeace Canada can assist investors in making their views known to management (addresses in appendix 3).

It is possible for a shareholder to assign a proxy to these groups at the annual meeting of a company. This means that the shareholder group will actually vote on your behalf if you are unable to attend the meeting.

In other cases, an investor may want to join with a shareholder organization in actually sponsoring a resolution to secure information from management or change objectionable practices. Individuals may also speak on their own behalf at shareholder meetings.

ALTERNATIVE INVESTMENTS

As mentioned previously, alternative investment is distinguished from ethical investment *per se* because alternative investment seeks out particular types of enterprises, rather than screening investment according to certain social standards. Alternative investment is sometimes known as "community investment" because of its concern with community well-being.

The Institute for Community Economics (ICE), a Massachusetts-based community loan fund and the largest community fund in the U.S., says that community-based investment involves three essential commitments:

- It seeks to strengthen the networks of mutual support that exist within a local community.
- It seeks to alter the priorities that determine the allocation of capital within the community, placing the highest rather than the lowest priority on the capital needs of those who have been exploited or excluded by prevailing economic forces.
- It supports community-based institutions that promote economic justice and strengthen the economic base of the local community.

As ICE says "Community investment thus channels capital into non-profit and worker-owned businesses rather than into companies owned by non-working shareholders, and into community land trusts and limited-equity housing cooperatives rather than into conventionally-owned land and housing, with their vulnerability to speculation and absentee ownership."

Canadian alternative- and community-investment opportunities are not as far advanced as they are in the United States, but it is an area that is attracting growing attention from social and political activists in this country.

Community-Investment Funds

One of the most common ways in which local capital is channelled into community enterprises in Canada is through community-investment funds. These funds operate much like stock-market mutual funds, except that investments are restricted to certain types of enterprises in certain localities. Investors contribute cash to the fund, and the fund manager lends that money directly to the enterprises.

While it is not strictly called a community-investment fund, the largest fund in the country investing in community economic development is the Quebec Federation of Labour Solidarity Fund, discussed earlier in this chapter.

The Solidarity Fund has raised $95 million from 41,000 investors in the province — 60 per cent of whom are members of unions affiliated with the Q.F.L. — to direct toward loans and equity interests in Quebec companies. Among the enterprises financed by the Solidarity Fund are a firetruck manufacturer, a manufacturer of wooden toys, a producer of educational softwear for children and a biotechnology company.

These kinds of enterprises are consonant with the Solidarity Fund commitment to create and maintain jobs in Quebec, to increase the influence of workers in the economic development of the province and to stimulate the Quebec economy through strategic investments (see appendix 4).

Other community investment funds are also available in certain centres across the country.

In Ottawa, a group of community activists converted a local college-education fund into CommunityWorks, a loan fund to provide financing to local businesses in eastern Ontario. CommunityWorks says that its primary objective "is to promote the growth and development of non-profit cooperatives and other community-owned businesses." Most of its financing has come from the former educational fund, but CommunityWorks is prepared to considered investments from individuals. For information on CommunityWorks, write to the fund at the address in appendix 8.

In Ontario, the Co-Operative Resource Pool of Ontario (CRPO) accepts money from individual investors and lends it to cooperative enterprises in need of financial assistance. CRPO invites investors to discuss the terms of their investment, along with the kinds of enterprises the investment could help finance. To obtain information on CRPO, contact Brian Iler at the address in appendix 8. Iler is a lawyer specializing in labour and cooperative law.

In Burnaby, British Columbia, a group of women have formed a fund known as the Women's Community Economic Development Loan Guarantee Fund in conjunction with the CCEC Credit Union in Vancouver. The fund accepts deposits from individuals and groups. The money is used to guarantee loans to women to "set up projects that meet the criteria for community economic development." Contributions to the fund can take the form of donations, deposits with the credit union with interest donated to the fund, or deposits with interest. To obtain information on the fund, write to the address in appendix 8.

In addition to these funds, some local communities have job-creation committees raising funds for local small business. These committees, operating under the federal government's Canadian Jobs Strategy program, solicit money for investments in job-creating enterprises. Under the terms of the program, the committees are established only in communities that are designated as economically distressed by the federal Department of Employment and Immigration.

Known as Community Futures or Local Employment and Development committees, the committees are funded by the federal government to a certain level; but the government's objective is gradually to place them on a self-sustaining basis.

Only a small number of these committees are soliciting private funds, but you can obtain information on your local job-creation committee by writing to the Canadian Jobs Strategy at the address in appendix 3.

Investments in community-investment funds are considered to carry a moderate-to-high risk, so they should be considered only by fairly enterprising investors, and investors willing to accept this level of risk.

Credit Unions and Other Alternative Institutions

As discussed in the previous chapters on credit unions and RRSPs, cooperative financial institutions serve to channel capital into local investments in a number of ways. The *caisses populaires* connected with the Desjardins group in Quebec, and the CCEC and Bread and Roses credit unions in English Canada are the leaders in this area; but there are other credit unions active in community economic development. For information on the Desjardins group, write to the address in appendix 1. For information on CCEC and Bread and Roses, write to the addresses in appendix 8.

There is also at least one trust company, Alberta-based Peace Hills Trust Co., which is active in the development of native-Canadian business. With 1986 assets of $100 million, Peace Hills describes itself as Canada's only Indian-owned, full-service trust company in Canada. It serves natives and non-natives from three offices — in Hobbema, Alberta, Edmonton and Winnipeg. Among other types of loans, the company lends mortgage money to Indian bands to improve housing on reserves. It also supports programs to encourage the development of native businesses, artists and entertainers. The company is owned by the Samson Indian band in Alberta.

As an investor, you may not be able to target specific kinds of investments with a deposit in one of these institutions. But supporting these institutions helps them to continue their community-economic development work.

Third World Investments

The Ecumenical Development Society of Hamilton (EDCS), Ontario, is the first Canadian branch of the Ecumenical Development Co-operative Society of Amersfoort, Netherlands. EDCS describes itself as a development bank. It is run by Christians and makes funds available to poor people wherever there is need. Most of the funds are directed to Third World countries, however. The main operating principle of EDCS is the biblical passage "If you give a fish to a hungry man you feed him for a day, but if you teach him how to fish you will feed him for a lifetime." The projects funded by EDCS are cooperative self- help projects, which would not receive funding through private banks. Some of the projects funded by EDCS include: a Turkish beekeeping enterprise providing benefits to 3,100 small farmers; an animal-feed mill in the Ivory Coast benefiting forty families; and an alpaca knitting cooperative in Peru that helps to support twelve hundred Inca families.

Individuals cannot buy directly into the parent organization, but they can invest in the Hamilton affiliate by purchasing shares at $250 each. At the time of writing (1987), the Hamilton affiliate was the only Canadian branch of the society. EDCS has paid a dividend of 2 per cent on its shares during the last two years.

For further information about EDCS, write to the address in appendix 8.

Worker Cooperative Investments

There are between three and four hundred worker-owned cooperative enterprises in Canada. Quebec is by far Canada's leader in worker cooperatives, accounting for about two hundred and seventy of the total. An estimated sixty-five worker cooperatives are operating in the province's forest industry alone.

With large multinational resource industries pulling out of many of Canada's mining and forest regions, governments and investors are looking for a viable alternative to provide jobs and income for depressed areas. Worker cooperatives often fit the bill. Business analysts estimate that between 70 and 80 per cent of all new conventional small businesses fail, while the corresponding figure for worker cooperatives is only about 20 per cent.

Several provinces have venture-capital loan programs for worker cooperatives, but there are ways that private investors can participate in these enterprises as well. As mentioned in the chapter on RRSPs, some worker cooperatives have been issuing preferred shares in the last few years to attract private debt capital to their enterprises without surrendering the democratic ownership that distinguishes them from conventional small businesses. One of the best-known examples of this kind of investment occurred with The Big Carrot in Toronto, a worker cooperative food store that raised more than $200,000 to help build a mall for itself and other innovative businesses.

To find worker cooperatives that are in need of financing, you should contact one of a number of resource organizations that do consultancy work for cooperative enterprises. These resource organizations are discussed in more detail in chapter 7.

U.S. Community-Loan Funds
While most investors concerned about community development will have an attachment to their own community, some others may be interested in community-investment funds in the United States. The largest of these, mentioned earlier, is the Institute for Community Economics. You can get information on other U.S. community funds by writing to the National Association of Community Development Loan Funds, based in Greenfield, Massachusetts (address in appendix 8).

Worker Buyouts
Not only are the number of worker cooperatives growing, but the numbers of failing companies purchased by their employees is also on the rise. Three of the largest employee takeovers during the last fifteen years in Canada have been the purchase of the Canadian International Paper Co. mill in Temiscaming, Quebec, in 1972; the buyout of Northern Breweries, Sault Ste-Marie, Ontario, from Carling-O'Keefe in 1977; and the takeover of Swift Eastern meat packers in Toronto from Gainers in 1985.

While employees facing a plant closure may throw up their hands at the seeming impossibility of buying out the company, there *is* a way of taking over a company with a relatively small amount of cash. This technique, called a "leveraged buyout," is a process whereby the employees, or any other group of investors, acquire a company with a small downpayment and a large amount of debt, backed by the assets of the company and the personal guarantees of the purchasers.

For information on worker buyouts, you should contact the Worker Ownership Development Foundation (address in appendix 3).

4

TAXATION — USING TAX DOLLARS TO DO GOOD

During the 1984 federal election, New Democratic Party leader Ed Broadbent drove the issue of tax avoidance to the front pages of the nation's newspapers. He rallied public anger at the fact that more than 8,000 Canadians earning $50,000 or more could get away with paying no tax by using shelters, investment loopholes and other tax dodges.

That campaign helped to bring ordinarily sleep-inducing matters of taxation to public attention. A widespread debate was launched on the following question. From the viewpoint of the public — not the investor — is it appropriate to use tax shelters to achieve policy objectives if they result in an unfair tax system that benefits high-income taxpayers?

This question is a very personal issue for ethical investors. On the one hand, like other middle- and high-income Canadians, they stand to benefit from tax incentives that are less accessible to lower-income taxpayers. On the other hand, they well know that these incentives help them to promote social well-being through ethical investments.

The use of ethical tax incentives does not totally resolve the ethical problem of the tax system. After all, ethical investors with enough money to put toward investment tax incentives still stand to benefit personally from the tax system. However, a careful choice of these tax incentives based on ethical criteria will ensure that public tax funds are employed with the best social considerations in mind.

In addition, there are some tax provisions, such as deductions for political or charitable contributions, which provide no direct benefit to the taxpayer. Instead, these incentives encourage socially minded taxpayers to open their pockets for particular causes. A portion of the contribution is offset by lower taxes, but the contributor does not stand to gain any income in return for his or her contribution.

To people who have never invested a dime in a tax shelter, this entire topic may seem somewhat esoteric. But tax planning is not only for those with big money. There are plenty of tax measures — which carry important ethical considerations — that are easily accessible to the majority of taxfilers. This chapter will discuss these measures along with some of the ethically important shelters and incentives open to taxpayers with more sophisticated needs.

INTRODUCTION TO THE TAX FORM

Before discussing tax measures that have special ethical significance, it is important to gain an understanding of some of the basic tax exemptions, deductions and credits.

You may be reading this book for help in filling out your 1987 tax return. Or you may be looking for help in planning your 1988 taxes. In either case, one of the most important things to keep in mind is that your taxes in 1988 are going to look very different from your taxes in 1987. Your 1988 return is going to be changed to reflect the tax-reform measures unveiled on June 18, 1987, by federal Finance Minister Michael Wilson in his White Paper on taxation.

This White Paper is a rundown of the measures that the government intends to introduce beginning in the 1988 tax year. At the time of writing (1987), these measures were still in the proposal stage, and may be altered before you receive your tax returns at the end of 1988. But the government stated clearly that it intends to enact the major reforms set out in the paper.

As explained in the chapter on RRSPs, income is taxed according to a "ladder" of rates, the highest of which is called your marginal rate of taxation. Your lowest block of income is taxed at a very low rate, while the next is taxed at a higher rate, and the next at a still higher rate, and so on. One of the most important objectives for taxpayers is to reduce taxable income. Not only does this directly reduce your tax payable but it can reduce the bracket at which your top income is taxed.

The following charts set out approximate 1987 tax brackets, and approximate proposed 1988 brackets. These brackets are approximate since every province charges its own rate of taxation as a percentage of the basic federal tax.

Table 7

Federal/Provincial Income Tax, 1987

Taxable income $	Approx. marginal rate %
1,318 or less	9
1,319 to 2,638	24
2,639 to 5,278	25.5
5,279 to 7,917	27
7,918 to 13,196	28.5
13,197 to 18,475	30
18,476 to 23,754	34.5
23,755 to 36,951	37.5
36,952 to 63,346	45
63,347 and over	51

Table 8

Federal/Provincial Income Tax, 1988

Taxable income $	Approx. marginal rate %
up to 27,500	25.5
27,501 to 55,000	39
55,001 and over	43.5

Under the White Paper proposals, the number of brackets is to be reduced from ten to three and the marginal rate of taxation will be reduced. Because the marginal rates are lower, the government will receive less revenue. To help recoup some of this lost revenue, the government proposes to introduce an expanded federal sales tax.

Your 1987 Taxes

Here is a rundown of the basic exemptions and deductions for 1987.

Table 9

Basic Exemptions and Deductions, 1987

Basic personal	$4,220
Age 65 and over	$2,640
Pension	up to $1,000
Married	up to $3,700
Dependants under 18	up to $560
Dependants 18 and over	up to $1,200
Dependants 18 and over and mentally or physically infirm	up to $1,450
Equivalent to married[1]	up to $3,700
Disability	$2,890
Education	$50 for each month you were a full-time student

[1]This is often mistaken as a married deduction for spouses living in a common-law relationship. In fact, the equivalent-to-married exemption may be claimed if you were single, divorced, separated or widowed and you supported a relative by blood, marriage or adoption who lived with you. It can apply to single people supporting a child, parent, grandparent, sibling or in-law. While you cannot claim a common- law spouse, you can claim a child if you live in a common-law relationship.

If you have such a low income that your age and pension reduce your taxable income to less than zero, you may want to transfer them to your spouse. If you do not earn enough to use completely the disability or education deductions, you may be able to transfer them to your spouse or supporting person. The guide included with your tax form gives instructions on how to transfer exemptions.

Your 1988 Taxes

For 1988, the White Paper proposes to change the above system of exemptions and deductions to credits. The following figures — estimates that will vary from province to province — will then apply:

Table 10

Basic "Credits," 1988

Personal	$1,580
Age 65 and over	$850
Married	up to $1,315
Pension	up to $170
Dependants under 18	up to $100
Dependants 18 and over	Nil
Dependants 18 and over and mentally or physically infirm	$385
Equivalent to married	up to $1,315
Disability	$850
Education	$10 for each month you were a full-time student

You will note that the tax credits are much lower than the exemptions. However, keep in mind that credits are the actual dollar amount that will be subtracted from your tax payable — the amount you are required to submit to Revenue Canada. Exemptions are used to reduce taxable income — the amount used to calculate your tax payable. An exemption is of greater value to a taxpayer in a high tax bracket than someone in a low tax bracket. Credits are of the same value regardless of tax bracket.

For example, a taxpayer in a 37-per-cent tax bracket would save $1,561 because of the $4,220 personal exemption, while a taxpayer in a 25-per-cent bracket would save $1,055. With the proposed 1988 personal tax credit, both taxpayers would save $1,580.

Unused portions of these credits will not be refunded to taxfilers who have no tax to pay. In other words, in order to receive these credits you must earn enough income to pay taxes. However, the age and pension credits can be transferred to your spouse and the disability and education credits can be transferred to your spouse or supporting parent or grandparent.

These lists are only a partial rundown of the exemptions, deductions and credits available to taxfilers. You should carefully check the general tax guide and return for your province to ensure that you are making use of all possible tax measures.

POLITICAL CONTRIBUTIONS

Fortunately, for ethically minded taxfilers, one of the most accessible tax measures — the political-contributions credit — is also one with considerable ethical implications.

The political-contributions credit is a rebate of a portion of the contributions that taxpayers make to a registered political party or candidate. You can claim a credit against federal taxes payable for contributions to federal parties or candidates, or — in British Columbia, Alberta, Manitoba, Ontario, Quebec, Nova Scotia, New Brunswick and the Yukon — you can claim a credit against provincial taxes for contributions made to provincial parties or candidates.

Of all the measures available to help reduce individual taxes, the political-contributions credit is one of the most generous. The federal credit is 75 per cent of the first $100 contributed, plus 50 per cent of the next $450, plus 33.3 per cent of the amount exceeding $550, up to a maximum credit of $500. Thus, if you contribute $150, you will have a $100 credit toward your federal tax payable. Two-thirds of your total contribution will be financed by the tax system.

British Columbia, Manitoba, New Brunswick, Nova Scotia, Prince Edward Island and the Yukon have similar political-contribution credits. Alberta provides a credit of 75 per cent for the first $150, 50 per cent for the next $675 and 33.3 per cent over $875 up to a maximum credit of $750. Ontario provides 75 per cent of the first $200, 50 per cent of the next $600 and 33.3 per cent over $800 up to a maximum credit of $750. Quebec provides a credit of 50 per cent for a contribution up to $280, up to a maximum credit of $140.

At the federal level, a registered party is a party represented in the House of Commons, or one which had at least fifty candidates nominated for the federal election. These requirements mean that you can receive a credit for contributions to the three main parties, the Liberal Party of Canada, the New Democratic Party of Canada and the Progressive Conservative Party of Canada. As of June 24, 1987, the following were also registered political parties: the Communist Party of Canada, the Confederation of Regions Western Party, the Green Party of Canada, the Libertarian Party of Canada, the Social Credit Party of Canada, Le Parti Nationaliste du Québec, Le Parti Rhinoceros and the Party for the Commonwealth of Canada.

To receive a current list of registered parties and their addresses, or other information on the Canada Elections Act, write to Elections Canada (address in appendix 3).

The ethical considerations of political party contributions cannot be overstated. The *raison d' être* of the political-contribution credit is to encourage ordinary Canadian taxfilers to contribute to the party of their choice. Not only does this contribution help to enliven the political commitment of average Canadians, it helps to reduce the influence of corporations and large private-interest groups in our political system.

From a financial point of view, there are a number of things to keep in mind. If you are a relatively low-income taxpayer, you may not be able to get a large credit for political contributions. This is because any political-contribution credit in excess of the amount required to reduce your federal tax to zero is not refundable. If, on the other hand, you have sufficient income to use the credit, you should contribute in the most tax-efficient way possible.

If you want to make a large contribution, say for an election campaign, you should consider splitting your contribution over two years. For example, a single $200 federal contribution in one year would return a credit of $125, while two annual contributions of $100 would return $150. In addition, if you want to make a large contribution, you should consider splitting it between the federal and provincial parties in your jurisdiction. This way you can claim political-contribution credits against your federal and provincial tax payable. A $100 contribution to a federal party would return a $75 federal tax credit and a $100 Ontario contribution would return a $75 provincial credit, for a total tax saving of $150.

If you are married, and if you have insufficient income to use the federal or Ontario credits, your spouse can claim the contributions on his or her tax return. In Ontario, you should also keep in mind that you have to subtract provincial property and sales tax credits from your provincial political-contribution credits.

CHARITABLE CONTRIBUTIONS

The tax benefit of contributions to charities is small compared with the incentive given to political contributions, but many ethically minded taxpayers still find charitable donations worthwhile for social and financial reasons.

In order to qualify for a tax deduction on your donation, donors must contribute to a registered charity, of which there are thousands in Canada. A registered charity is a non-profit organization constituted for charitable purposes and approved for charitable status by Revenue Canada. Registered charities are entitled to issue tax recipts to donors, who may use them to claim income tax deductions.

The law on charities is centuries old, dating to the English Statute of Elizabeth in 1601, which defined charities in terms of activities such as aged and poor relief, help for the ill, repair of ports and highways, maintenance of jails, aid to tradesmen and relief and rehabilitation of prisoners. These traditional definitions have spawned such health charities as the Canadian Cancer Society, the Canadian Heart Foundation and the Canadian Diabetic Association, and relief charities such as Help the Aged, Goodwill Industries and Children's Aid Societies.

The common law on charities restricts the amount of political activity that they may carry out. Charities that are involved in political issues must be mindful that they could lose their charitable status if they offend this prohibition. Some charities, like the Canadian Civil Liberties Association, have split themselves in two — into clearly political organizations that cannot grant tax deductions, and educational organizations that are registered charities. Recent clarifications to Revenue Canada rules have, however, given charitable organizations more freedom.

The federal government's May 1985 budget announced that charities would be able to become involved in limited political activity. In February 1987, Revenue Canada issued an information circular setting out this policy. It stated that political activities that are "subordinate to bona fide charitable purposes" will be permitted within certain spending limits. This means that charities may sponsor publications, conferences, workshops, advertising, lawful demonstrations or mailing campaigns to sway public opinion on political issues. This said, charities are still prohibited from directly or indirectly endorsing or opposing a specific candidate or political party. Also, a charity must spend no more than 10 per cent of its resources on political activities.

These rules are expected to encourage charities to become more vocal on social and political issues, a welcome development for ethically minded charitable donors.

Tax reforms proposed in the June 1987 White Paper are also expected to make charitable contributions more attractive for low- and middle-income people. Under current rules, donors to registered charities may claim an exemption of up to 20 per cent of net income.

Effective in the 1988 tax year, the White Paper proposes to change this to a federal tax credit of 17 per cent for the first $250 of your charitable donation and 29 per cent in excess of $250. The White Paper says that the change will benefit many lower- and middle-income tax filers who donate more than $250 in a year, and will create a greater incentive for charitable giving.

At the time of writing (1987), charitable organizations were lobbying the federal Department of Finance to lower the $250 threshold and provide refundability of the credit — two measures that would distinctly be of assistance to low-income Canadians.

If you are considering making a charitable contribution, the Better Business Bureau of Metropolitan Toronto suggests the following guidelines for donating (if you want to check to determine whether a particular charity is reputable, you can ask your local BBB):

- Learn about the principles of the soliciting organization. A federal income tax registration is no guarantee that the charity is a good cause.
- Legitimate solicitors and agencies do not use high-pressure methods to force you to give before you are able to make inquiries.
- If a solicitor refuses to show you identification, do not contribute.
- Remember that names of contributors are sometimes flashed to impress you. This does not necessarily mean that all of the persons know that their names are being used.
- The use of a well-respected group's name is no assurance that the promoter running a fund-raising drive is legitimate. These groups have often been misled by promoters.
- Never agree to contribute in response to a telephone call. Ask for a letter or annual report.
- Never pay in cash. Write a cheque made payable to the organization.
- Get an official receipt, including taxation number, if you want a tax exemption or credit.

INVESTMENTS

Investors — both ethical and traditional — in Canadian companies can gain significant benefits through the federal tax system, especially if their investments generate dividends. Three of the most important aspects of the federal tax system for investors concern the taxation of dividends, interest and capital gains. If the White Paper proposals are implemented, these measures will be eliminated, or scaled back, in 1988.

In the following discussion, keep in mind that these tax incentives pertain to interest, dividends or capital gains generated on investments held outside of an RRSP. If you earn income *within* an RRSP, the income is tax-free until you withdraw it — at which point it is taxed at your marginal rate of taxation.

Interest Income

In 1987 and previous tax years, investors could claim an interest and dividend income deduction of up to $1,000 from their taxable income if they earned income from dividends, bonds, investment certificates, term deposits or other interest-bearing investments. This was used by many elderly people, for example, who earn substantial interest income from retirement savings. The tax reform White Paper proposes to eliminate this deduction for the 1988 tax year.

Dividends

Income from dividends earned from taxable Canadian corporations is taxed a lower rate than income from wages, interest or other sources. On the face of it, this may seem unfair. However, Revenue Canada takes the position that dividends are given to shareholders from the after-tax profits of Canadian companies. Since the profit has already been taxed at the corporate level, Revenue Canada maintains that it is not necessary to tax it at the individual level at the same rate as other income.

For 1987 taxes, the following is the way dividends will be taxed. When you receive a dividend from a corporation, you are required to report it as income on your tax return. You will then be required to increase it by an additional 33.3 per cent — which is known as a dividend "gross-up." The grossed-up dividend is taxed at your marginal rate. This appears to be a penalty rather than an incentive for declaring dividends as income. However, you are also able to claim a dividend tax credit, which is equal to 33.3 per cent of your initial dividend. By directly reducing your tax payable, this dividend tax credit more than compensates you for the increase in taxable income generated by the dividend gross-up.

For 1988, however, the tax reform White Paper proposes a higher rate of taxation for dividends. It maintains that dividends should be taxed at a higher rate because corporate tax rates are being lowered as part of the tax-reform package.

Table 11

How to Calculate Your Dividend Tax Credit
(assumes provincial tax rate 50 per cent of federal rate, top rate equals 51% in 1987, 43.5% in 1988)

	1987	1988
Dividend	$100.00	$100.00
Gross-up	$33.33	$25.00
Additional taxable income	$133.33	$125.00
Tax payable at top rate	$68.00	$54.38
Dividend tax credit	$33.33	$25.00
Net tax payable	$34.67	$29.38
Tax payable if earned in wages or interest	$51.00	$43.50
Tax saved from dividends	$16.33	$14.12

The White Paper proposals mean that in 1988 you will have to gross-up your initial dividend by 25 per cent, not 33.3 per cent as in 1987. This grossed-up dividend will then be taxed at your marginal rate. The dividend tax credit that you will be able to claim will be 25 per cent, however, not 33.3 per cent as in 1987.

As well, the White Paper proposes reducing the top marginal tax rate, so comparisons in the changes to the dividend tax credit become a little complicated. But at the top tax bracket of 51 per cent in 1987, and 43.5 per cent in 1988, you can see that there is less of a saving to top-tax-paying income-earners in 1988 than in 1987. In 1987, top-income earners save $16.33 in taxes for every $100 in dividend income compared with other income, while in 1988 they will save $14.12.

Capital gains

Capital gains are the gain in the value of property after the property is sold. For example, if stock is purchased for $10 a share and sold for $15, the capital gain is $5 per share. While capital gains apply to different kinds of property, including art work, coins, condominiums and cottages, the most likely kind of ethical investment to which it would apply is corporate stock.

In 1985, the federal government proposed to exempt from taxation capital gains up to $500,000 during a taxpayer's lifetime. The exemption was to be phased in over a period of five years, so the full $500,000 figure would not be reached until the 1990 tax year.

In the June 1987 White Paper, the federal government announced that it would cap the exemption at $100,000. This is the level the scheduled exemption reached in 1987. In 1987 and subsequent years, taxpayers will be able to claim a lifetime capital gain of $100,000 without paying tax. In 1987, 50 per cent of any capital gains over and above the $100,000 exemption must be included as income. In 1988, this becomes two-thirds, and in 1990, it changes to three-quarters.

Mutual Funds

Mutual funds that hold stock-market shares are generally treated the same as stock for tax purposes. This means that unit-holders will receive a yearly form from their mutual fund detailing any dividends or capital gains earned by the fund. The dividend tax-credit and capital-gains exemptions can be claimed for these sources of income. In 1987, you will also be able to claim the $1,000 interest and dividend deduction. When you sell your units you can also claim the capital-gains exemption to avoid paying tax on the increase in unit value.

Borrowing for Investments

Revenue Canada permits taxpayers to deduct from their taxable income interest expenses on loans and other carrying charges incurred in the purchase of stock, bonds or other investments. However, interest on loans used to purchase investments for a registered retirement savings plan (RRSP) is not deductible.

Provincial Incentives

Several provincial governments offer stock-savings plans designed to encourage residents to invest in companies based in those provinces, or which employ large numbers of people in those provinces.

The former Parti Québécois government introduced the Quebec Stock Savings Plan (QSSP), the first provincial stock plan in Canada, in 1979. The QSSP permits Quebec taxpayers to deduct investments in stock of companies based in Quebec, or which pay more than 50 per cent of all wages in Quebec. The deduction limit is $5,500, or 10 per cent of income. There are additional rules governing the amount of deductions for stock in large, medium and emerging companies.

The Saskatchewan Stock Savings Tax Credit program gives taxpayers a tax credit of 30 per cent of the cost of eligible shares to a maximum of $3,000. In order to qualify, shares must be purchased in companies that pay at least 25 per cent of their total wages in Saskatchewan. Taxpayers must hold the stock for the remainder of the tax year, plus two more years.

The Alberta Stock Savings Plan provides tax credits of between 10 and 30 per cent up to a maximum $3,000. The shares must be purchased in companies listed on the Alberta Stock Exchange.

Nova Scotia also introduced a stock-savings plan in June 1987, but at the time of writing (1987) no companies were yet included within the plan. In order to qualify, the companies must have a place of business in Nova Scotia, and pay at least 25 per cent of their wages in the province. Taxpayers who invest in such companies are eligible for a 20- or 30-per-cent tax credit, up to a maximum of $3,000.

TAX AND ETHICAL INVESTMENTS

This rundown of tax investment incentives shows clearly that the tax system favours equity investments over interest-bearing investments. This is becoming increasingly the case with the elimination of the $1,000 interest and dividend deduction with the 1988 tax year.

Interest-bearing investments — such as term deposits, guaranteed investment certificates and government or corporate bonds — are attractive to investors who want a secure rate of return and a guarantee that they will not lose their capital. Unfortunately, the tax treatment of these vehicles is inferior to stock-market investments or mutual funds that hold stock-market shares. In order to defer paying tax on the income generated from these investments, it is necessary to purchase these investments inside a registered retirement savings plan (RRSP).

One tradeoff in this dilemma that is becoming attractive to many ethical investors is to find a company that offers preferred shares and fits their ethical "screens." Preferred shares offer a set dividend, which is eligible for the dividend tax credit; but share prices are generally less volatile than common stock. However, it is important to remember that preferred share dividends are not guaranteed, even if companies are obliged to pay preferred dividends before they make a payout to common shareholders.

SPECIAL INCENTIVES AND ETHICAL INVESTMENT

In addition to these general tax measures, federal and provincial governments offer tax shelters or other incentives to encourage investors to place capital in particular kinds of enterprises. While many of these deal with speculative investments, such as oil or mining exploration ventures, there are also some which appeal specifically to ethically oriented investors.

Cooperative Enterprises

Worker cooperatives and credit unions justifiably complain that the tax system is unfairly biased in favour of private-sector investments and against investments in cooperatives. This is particularly the case when you consider the impact of the capital-gains exemption. The capital-gains exemption permits people holding equity in an enterprise to earn tax-free income from any increase in the value of that equity. Shares held by workers in a cooperative or members of a credit union are always the same value because there is no market in which they are traded. The result is that cooperative enterprises are severely limited in their ability to raise capital, and this handicap is aggravated by the tax incentives given to equity investors.

The Co-operative Union of Canada, the national association of cooperatives and credit unions, is lobbying the federal government for special tax measures to address this particular problem in cooperative financing. Representatives of the cooperative movement have received a favourable hearing from federal officials. However, one province — Quebec — has already acted to help rectify this tax bias.

In 1985, the Quebec government introduced a plan called the Cooperative Investment Plan (CIP), which provides tax incentives for investments in eligible producing, processing, agricultural or worker's cooperatives by members or employees of those cooperatives. Taxpayers are able to claim a deduction from taxable income of up to $5,500 — or 10 per cent of total income. If you claim deductions under other investment incentives, such as the Quebec Stock Savings Plan or the Fonds de solidarité des travailleurs du Québec, your deduction may be reduced.

In order to qualify, the investment must be in preferred shares. Preferred shares are specified because the cooperative is not legally bound to pay interest, as in a bond — and preferred shares do not affect control of the enterprise, as common stocks do.

Labour-Sponsored Venture-Capital Funds
The Quebec and Saskatchewan governments have enacted special tax incentives for investors in labour-sponsored funds raising venture capital. Venture capital is used to finance relatively young or small enterprises. In 1987, the Quebec Federation of Labour Solidarity Fund (Fonds de solidarité des travailleurs du Québec) was the only eligible fund.

Contributions to the Solidarity Fund are eligible for a Quebec tax credit of 20 per cent of the shares purchased, up to a maximum of $700, and a 20-per-cent matching federal credit, up to an additional $700. These credits reduce tax payable. There is further information on the Solidarity Fund in the previous chapter on investments.

Venture-Capital Corporations
British Columbia, Saskatchewan, and Quebec offer tax incentives to investors in corporations which raise venture capital for small, emerging business. The programs are available for corporations raising money for such enterprises as manufacturing, processing, tourism, research and agricultural companies. In Ontario, the provincial government pays investors in qualified so-called Small Business Development Corporations a tax-free cash grant equal to 25 per cent of their investment.

However, there are serious ethical and financial considerations to take into account with these incentives. Venture-capital corporations usually specify the type of enterprises in which they will invest, but they do not apply social screens to their investments. As a result, you have no assurance that your money will be invested according to social criteria.

Financially, it is important to keep in mind that shares in many of these corporations are not traded on stock markets or over-the-counter markets (the markets for private securities transactions). This means that they may be exceedingly difficult to sell when you want your money back. In addition, you should remember that these special programs are set up to encourage investors to place money in high-risk companies. While you may be eligible for tax incentives or cash grants, you will have to accept a high level of risk.

Tax Shelters

Tax shelters permit investors in specified industries to deduct losses in those industries against other income. Revenue Canada permits investors in these industries to claim losses against their income because it wants to encourage investment. Generally, shelters are permitted in industries in the start-up phase, before these industries begin to generate revenue and profits. Two of the most popular types of tax shelters are Canadian films and resource-exploration ventures in the petroleum and mining industries.

From a financial point of view, many tax shelters present the same problems as venture capital corporations, namely high risk and lack of liquidity. Because it may be hard for you to sell these tax-shelter investments, the prospectus often contains a warning like this: "There is no market for the units, so it may be difficult or even impossible for the limited partners to sell them."

However, for investors who are interested in the Canadian film industry, film shelters may be an ethically satisfying and financially rewarding place in which to invest. They offer the investor the knowledge that he or she is contributing to the Canadian film industry (although many of the films produced under tax shelters have been thrashed by critics as utter schlock). In addition, they offer attractive incentives.

For 1987, the federal government permits investors with an interest in a certified Canadian production (a qualified film) to claim 50 per cent of their investment in each of two years. In order to qualify, the certified film must complete its principal photography in the first year.

However, for 1988, the White Paper proposes to severely cut this incentive. It recommends that deductions in certified films be limited to 30 per cent of the investment. After the White Paper was issued, the film industry lobbied the federal government to increase this limit.

In regard to resource-exploration ventures, there are two ways of viewing whether or not these enterprises are "ethical" investments.

On the one hand, these tax shelters help to provide capital for drilling companies operating in remote areas of the country. They provide jobs and income to regions that would not otherwise be able to support viable industries. These companies, known as junior exploration firms, carry out extremely risky activity that paves the way for the large mining and oil companies to establish profitable mines or oilfields. For example, the oil industry estimates that only one in ten exploratory holes in remote areas will turn into a commercial well.

On the other hand, ethical investors concerned about Canada's reliance on non-renewable resources may consider resource tax shelters more of a problem than a solution to Canada's economic difficulties. There are no similar tax shelters for solar energy, alternative energy (such as energy from waste) or energy conservation companies (such as wind generator manufacturers). Consequently, the federal tax system helps to draw capital toward non-renewable industries that create relatively few jobs for every dollar invested. In addition, there are serious environmental concerns about non-renewable resource industries.

Yet, if you are an investor who feels that resource industries pass your ethical screens, you may be interested in investing in one of many oil, gas or mining tax shelters. One of the most popular is so-called flow-through shares. These are shares of a junior exploration company — usually a mining venture, but some petroleum companies, too — in which losses by the company flow through directly to the shareholders and are deductible on their income. Taxpayers are eligible to deduct 100 per cent of the cost of flow-through shares. In addition, investors are eligible for a further Earned Depletion Allowance deduction. In 1987, the depletion allowance was 33.3 per cent of the investment in flow-through shares. This means that flow-through shares are actually worth a deduction of 133.3 per cent to the investor.

In the White Paper, the government proposed to reduce the Earned Depletion Allowance to 16.66 per cent after June 30, 1988, and to eliminate it entirely after June 30, 1989. This means that flow-through shares will be less attractive, but that they will still provide tax-shelter opportunities for aggressive investors in the resource industries.

Resource-industry investors may also be able to claim deductions on exploration or development expenses, as well as special provincial petroleum and mining incentives. Since these are extremely sophisticated shelters, it is best to purchase them through a broker knowledgable about the petroleum or mining industries.

PEACE TAX FUND

In Canada, the United States and other countries, people of conscience are beginning to withhold the portion of their taxes that goes toward military purposes. The practice is illegal but about four hundred Canadians are doing just that because of their fundamental opposition to war.

An organization called Conscience Canada — founded by a group of Quakers in Victoria, British Columbia — has set up the Canadian Peace Tax Fund, which accepts deposits from taxpayers who do not want to pay the proportion of their taxes that would otherwise go to military purposes. By depositing this money in a fund, these taxpayers are able to state categorically that their action is motivated by conscience, not by a desire to avoid paying taxes.

In addition to operating the fund, Conscience Canada has sponsored a court claim filed by Dr. Jerilynn Prior saying that taxpayers have a right under the Canadian Charter of Rights and Freedoms to withhold taxes earmarked for military purposes. Prior's claim specifically mentions article 2 of the charter, which states: "Everyone has the following fundamental freedoms: a) freedom of conscience and religion, b) freedom of thought, belief, opinion and expression." The case was scheduled to be heard in the Federal Court in the fall of 1987.

If you earn all of your income from wages or salaries, it is unlikely you will be able effectively to withhold a portion of your taxes, because your taxes are deducted at source by your employer. If you have a large portion of investment, pension or self-employed income, you have a better opportunity to withhold taxes. However, you must remember that, pending the outcome of the Prior case, withholding taxes may have serious consequences. Revenue Canada may deduct any taxes owing, plus interest, from subsequent rebates in future years, or require your employer to garnishee your wages — or it may start expensive collection proceedings.

If you would like to withhold your taxes, to support the Conscience Canada court case, or to obtain further information, you should write to Conscience Canada at the address listed in appendix 3.

5

TIME OFF — HOW TO START ENJOYING LIFE AGAIN

For millions of Canadians, the world of work is going to change dramatically in the near-future. The historic pattern — fifteen years of schooling, followed by forty-five years of employment (for men) or domestic work (for women), followed by a golden retirement — is on the way out. The traditional expectations about work are dissolving in the face of enormous shifts in the age makeup of our population, the rising aspirations of women and the deindustrialization of our economy.

The 1983 federal government report *Learning and Living* predicts that during the next twenty years "global industrial and employment restructuring, technological change, and the emerging leisure society will affect between four and eight million existing jobs, wiping out many and creating others." Many of these jobs will become temporary, contract or part-time jobs. Indeed, in the period between 1976 and 1982, part-time workers were the fastest-growing segment of the labour force.

This massive job change sounds frightening. Canadians will have less security than they had in the past, and many new jobs will have low pay and low benefits. But temporary jobs and less work time are not invariably bad in themselves.

Some Canadian workers want to take a leave of absence from work — or quit their jobs — to spend time with their children, return to school, enjoy an extended holiday, start their own business, or devote more time to volunteer for community activities. In some cases, these people are actually paid a salary (or receive government benefits) to take time off work. In many more cases, however, they must finance their time off through savings or investments.

Others are dropping from full-time jobs to part-time jobs, or job-sharing situations. Many of these people are mothers who want to spend more time at home without totally sacrificing the wages and benefits of paid work.

Still others are older employees who have spent a good part of their lives in the paid workforce, but want to leave before the traditional retirement age of sixty-five. More and more companies are giving early retirement bonuses to these workers, but many also have to find ways of providing for their own early pension income.

On the face of it, this emerging job situation sounds as if it is going to reduce the capabilities for ethical investment, rather than enlarge them. After all, a leave from work lowers the amount of income you have for ethical or conventional investments. But the ethical use of money concerns much more than investment only. It concerns how Canadians create and distribute their wealth, and whether their jobs help to create fulfilling work for all.

Some people contend that part-time jobs, educational and parental leaves and extended holidays do nothing more than spread under-employment to larger numbers of workers. There is some truth to this argument, and certainly flexible work arrangements are not for people — single mothers, for instance — who can barely make ends meet on a full-time salary. All the same, less work for people who can afford time off from their jobs holds the potential to create more work for people who cannot.

In addition, a reprieve from the drudgery of work will allow you to enjoy more fully your family, volunteer and community interests and personal enthusiasms. Parents will have more time to spend with their children, ex-students can return to school for personal or professional enrichment, and burned-out workers can start their own businesses, take part in volunteer activity or jump on a plane for a well-deserved holiday.

FINANCING A LEAVE FROM WORK

Saving from your income is the obvious but not the only way to finance a leave of absence. You can also spend RRSP savings or borrow against them; take out a loan; save in a registered education plan; defer a portion of your salary and collect the money when you are off the job; or negotiate a paid leave. The type of financing will vary according to how much you have saved, the length of time before you start your leave, the type of leave you are planning and contract arrangements with your employer.

Withdrawing from Your RRSP

One of the most common ways of financing a leave from work is with RRSPs. While some people may be able to negotiate paid leaves, and well-to-do investors can dip into their portfolios, RRSPs probably represent the best way for ordinary Canadians to take time off the job because RRSP savings are the only substantial fund of money they own.

As explained in the earlier chapter on RRSPs, you can withdraw money from these plans or collapse them completely before you retire. The problem, of course, is that you expose yourself to a heavy tax liability if you use your RRSP funds while you are still employed. However, if you withdraw money from your RRSP in a year when you take a leave, you will save in taxes because that RRSP money will be taxed at a lower-than-normal marginal rate.

The disadvantage to withdrawing RRSP money is that you are reducing your income-producing capacity for retirement. A withdrawal of money from your RRSP not only removes that amount, but it will remove all future gains on that amount earned from interest, dividends or capital gains. There are, however, differing views as to whether or not this is a serious problem. If you are young, and taking time off your job is important to you, it is probably worthwhile to take money out of your RRSP. Ultimately, this is a philosophical rather than a financial issue, but it makes little sense to stay in a job you dislike in order to provide income for a relatively affluent lifestyle sometime down the road.

In addition, you should make some forecast about your lifestyle after retirement. As mentioned in the RRSP chapter, financial planners estimate that many Canadians will have to accept a drop in income after retirement if they do not provide for their own pensions. This can be a serious problem for people who expect a conventional work-free retirement. However, many senior citizens in the future are expected to work on a part-time or on a contract basis, up to the time they die. This is especially true if healthy lifestyles improve the mental and physical capabilities of elderly people. If people continue to earn a wage or salary after they retire, there is less need for a huge retirement fund. This is especially true for retirees who live in homes that they own.

If you choose to withdraw money from your RRSP, there are a few considerations to keep in mind. First, timing your withdrawals to match periods of low income is essential for maximum tax savings. For instance, if you are taking a year off starting in September to enroll in school, it makes sense to try to live on your regular savings up to

January 1, and then dip into your RRSP funds in the new year. Otherwise your RRSP proceeds will be taxed at the relatively high marginal tax rate in the year in which you worked for eight months.

Secondly, keep in mind that Revenue Canada requires financial institutions to withhold a certain portion of RRSP funds for tax. For a withdrawal of less than $5,000, the tax is 10 per cent; for a withdrawal of $5,000 to $15,000, the amount is 20 per cent; and for withdrawals of more than $15,000, the tax is 30 per cent. This money will count as tax that has already been paid to Revenue Canada, but it makes sense to withdraw small RRSP amounts to ensure that maximum cash goes immediately to you, not the government. The only proviso on this is that you must check the RRSP withdrawal fees at your financial institution. These fees are about $25 a withdrawal at many institutions, and so many withdrawals can cost you dearly.

If you are planning to withdraw money from an RRSP, you will want to place your RRSP funds in fairly liquid investments, such as a bank account, treasury bills or term deposits. If you have a guaranteed investment certificate, you will have to wait until the end of the term, or sacrifice interest owing. If you have RRSP funds in stocks or bonds, you will have to sell those securities, which will cost you brokerage fees and the risk of selling at a loss.

If you do not want to use up your RRSP funds, there is a way of borrowing money from your RRSP. This makes sense if you intend to pay it back after you are working again. As mentioned in the chapter on RRSPs, it is possible for holders of a self-directed RRSP to use their funds to finance their own mortgage.

In this case, you can borrow money already in your RRSP. What you are doing is borrowing money from your RRSP and putting it in your mortgage. You will have to pay your RRSP a rate of return which is comparable to prevailing interest rates, and you will have to make arrangements to repay the principle. Under this arrangement, you put your house up as collateral to secure the loan you have taken from your RRSP. A trustee, such as a trust company, manages the arrangement to ensure that interest and principal are paid. (Futher details are provided in chapter 2 on RRSPs).

This may be a worthwhile arrangement for people who own their own homes, and are assured of steady income after their leave ends. Otherwise, you may go into default on your self-directed RRSP. Because the trustee is monitoring your payments, it is not possible to avoid paying interest and principal.

Another wrinkle in the RRSP regulations that may be of interest to some people concerns spousal RRSPs. As noted in chapter 2, Revenue Canada will allow people to contribute to the RRSP of their spouse. Ordinarily, this is done to equalize income in retirement. However, if you and your spouse are both working but your spouse intends to take a leave in four years or more, it might make sense to contribute to a spousal RRSP.

This way, your spouse — who will be on a leave in four years — will be able to draw on RRSP funds that will be larger than they would be if he or she were the only contributor. If you are trying to build up an RRSP fund in a hurry, this is one of the best ways to do it.

If you take this route, you should ensure that the leave will be taken in four years or longer. For if you withdraw money from an RRSP that has been contributed by your spouse, your spouse will be taxed on the withdrawal if he or she contributed within the last year or the previous two years. If you take a leave in four years, the spousal RRSP becomes taxable to *your* income, which will be lower because of the leave. While you are working, you can also contribute to your *own* RRSP, and you will have more RRSP money on which to draw for your leave than you would have if you were the only contributor.

Borrowing

If you are anxious to take a leave immediately, and you have no savings or investments, you will probably be forced to arrange the financing through borrowing. For many people, borrowing may make more sense than dipping into an RRSP. If you are taking a three- or four-month absence, for example, you may simply require a little extra cash to tide you over the tight period. In this case, it may not make sense to deplete your RRSP to get yourself through a short-term cash problem. This is especially the case if your RRSP is in stocks or other investments that may be costly to turn into cash.

If you choose to borrow, you should probably try to arrange a loan that has a term that is as long as possible, to ensure that the monthly payments are low while you are off the job. At the same time it might be a good idea to negotiate an open loan (which can be paid off at any time) so that when you return to work you can retire your debt as quickly as possible.

Savings or Investments

If you have bonds, term deposits, certificates or other interest-bearing investments, you will want to arrange your investments so that you do not have to report the interest until the year in which you take your leave. This way, it will be taxed at your lower marginal rate when you are earning less income.

There are several ways in which you can do this. One of the easiest is to purchase compound-interest Canada Savings Bonds. These are bonds that pay interest on the principal and past interest for a number of years. (They are readily distinguishable from regular interest bonds, which pay interest on the principal only.) After the first year, the bond-holder is guaranteed a minimum interest rate each year until maturity. These bonds can be easily purchased, by cash or monthly installments, through financial institutions or through payroll savings plans provided by many employers.

In addition, many financial institutions offer deposits or certificates that delay interest payments until the investment is mature.

You must keep in mind that Revenue Canada requires you to report interest income if it has accrued once every three years, *even if you have not received the cash.* You should therefore, start your investment planning three years before you intend to take your leave and try to forgo interest income in this period.

Tax planning for your interest-bearing investments is particularly important after 1987 because of the scheduled cancellation of the $1,000 interest and dividend deduction contained in the White Paper on tax reform. In 1987 and previous years it was possible to earn up to $1,000 in interest without adding it to your taxable income. For 1988 and subsequent years, however, the White Paper proposes to do away with this deduction.

Registered Education Savings Plans

Registered Education Savings Plans (RESPs), available at many investment dealers, pool monies contributed by subscribers that will earn income tax-free. Payments from these funds are made to students to assist them to further their education at the post-secondary level. Unlike RRSPs, investments in an RESP are not tax-deductible, but, like RRSPs, there is no tax on income earned by the fund.

Ordinarily, these funds are established by parents as a way to finance the university education of their children. But a beneficiary of an RESP may also be the subscriber. This means that people planning to take a leave to attend university are able to set up an RESP for themselves. Such a plan may be of interest to teachers, for example, who want to return to university at some point in the future to attain a graduate degree. Payments from an RESP are taxable in the hands of the beneficiary, so if you have a low income during your school year, the income tax bite will not be severe.

Salary Deferral Arrangements

The Income Tax Act contains a provision specially designed for people who wish to take time off the job in some future specified period. The act permits an employee — as long as the employer also agrees to the arrangement — to defer a portion of his or her salary for a set period, and then collect the money, with interest, during a leave of absence.

Called a salary-deferral arrangement, the idea has been slow to develop among private companies; but many school boards, community colleges, hospitals and other public sector agencies have embraced it. In a period of declining enrolments and social-service cutbacks, the salary-deferral plan has allowed many of these agencies to reduce their workforces without laying people off.

The concept is more than just a forced savings plan for employees. It gives them important tax benefits. Here is how it works. After an employer has agreed to grant an employee a leave of absence for a specified period at a particular time, the employer will set up a deferred-salary plan on behalf of the employee. The employee will then receive only a portion of his or her regular salary, and the rest will be deposited into the deferred plan. If an employee plans to take a leave in four years time, he or she would take a one-quarter salary cut for three years, get the fourth year off, and be paid all four years at three-quarters of regular salary.

Because the employer deposits the deferred portion of the salary in an interest-bearing investment, the employee will likely end up living on a higher salary than he or she had while working. This could come in handy if you have extra vacation expenses during your time off.

Under federal Finance Department regulations brought down in 1986, employees can defer up to 30 per cent of their salary per year, and the tax cannot be deferred longer than seven years. Any interest accumulating on the deferred salary will be taxed in the year it is accrued. In addition, employees must return to work for the same employer and return for a period at least equal to the amount of time off.

Deferred-salary plans are best for people who can plan their leave several years in advance. If you want just to pack up and leave in a month or two, they will not help. Perhaps more important, deferred-salary plans also require the approval of employers — which is not always, or even often, readily forthcoming.

The personnel director of one national company, when asked to institute a program of deferrred-salary plans, put it this way:

> Currently we consider requests for leaves based on their merits and requirements of operations. With a deferred plan, approval of leaves would have to be given four years in advance. It is difficult to plan operational requirements that far ahead. I also wonder how many individuals can plan leaves so far in advance. There would be extra administrative problems whenever a staffer on the deferred plan changed his or her mind and decided not to take the leave. I can think of many things, both personal and work-related, that might persuade someone not to take a planned leave.

Employees approaching their bosses about such a plan should understand that they will probably encounter more resistance than sympathy unless they work for one of a minority of progressive, enlightened employers. However, employees should stress that the administrative costs to the employer of such a plan are small compared with the benefits to be gained through improvement in employee morale. While only a few employees may make use of such a plan, employers can demonstrate that they care about their employees by instituting one.

Don Abrams, an instructor at Algonquin College in Ottawa, has written a book on deferred-salary plans called *The Time Buyer*. He has also organized a group called Don Abrams and Time-Buyer Associates (address in appendix 3), which can provide further information.

Paid (Maternity, Education) Leaves

Obviously, from the employee's point of view, paid leaves are the most advantageous kind of break from work. A whole or part-wage is still coming in during the time off, and the employee's savings are kept intact.

One kind of paid break from work is provided by the federal Unemployment Insurance Act for maternity or adoption leave. The Act will provide female employees with fifteen weeks of maternity benefits at 60 per cent of their normal wage. Unemployment benefits for fifteen weeks are also available to a parent who adopts a child. This means that, while you are not entitled to a full salary, you will get most of your regular salary paid by UIC. Many employees covered under collective agreements are also entitled to additional paid maternity leave.

Federal and provincial labour codes provide that female employees who have worked with an employer for a specified minimum period are eligible for an unpaid maternity leave. Your actual entitlement varies according to whether your company is regulated under federal or provincial jurisdiction. For most provinces, employees must have worked at least one year in order to qualify, and the leave is limited to seventeen or eighteen weeks. Employees in federal jurisdiction are entitled to twenty-four weeks' leave for the birth or adoption of a child. Several provinces also have provisions for adoption leave.

If you work for an employer under a collective agreement, you may be entitled to even longer periods of unpaid maternity or adoption leave. Even if you are not covered by a collective agreement, it may be possible to negotiate a longer period of unpaid time off.

Many women use vacation time, overtime owing or other time-off credits during their maternity leave as a way to finance their leave from work. This helps to meet the extra bills that a new child can create; but it could mean that you will have to wait a long time before you can take a holiday again.

Many employees may also be entitled to paid leave in order to take educational courses. In most cases the courses will have to be related to the employees' work, and approved by the employers.

Budget Considerations

The previous discussion has mentioned many of the tax consequences of particular ways of financing leaves of absence, but here are some financial considerations to keep in mind regardless of the way you finance your leave.

First, financial planners recommend that people maintain a cash fund for emergencies, even if they are on a leave of absence and money is tight. Ideally, this should be equal to between three and six months of your regular salary.

Second, the contract between your employer and the insurance company that funds your employee-benefit plan may have a provision allowing you to continue your benefits if you pay a weekly or monthly premium to your employer. You should have a careful look at your benefits and the cost required to maintain them. Many employee-benefit plans contain long-term disability benefits, life insurance, dental and drug plans, provincial health-insurance payments, eye-care benefits and other provisions. If you have good dental health and want to forgo disability and life insurance, it may be worthwhile not to pay for your company benefits. In this case, you will have to pay your provincial health-insurance premiums yourself, or switch them over to your spouse, if he or she has employer-paid premiums.

If you intend to travel outside of Canada for an extended period on your leave, you should notify your provincial health-insurance plan. You may also require private health insurance because provincial health insurance usually only covers treatment costs up to the amount specified in your province. If the cost of treatment exceeds that amount, you could get stuck with the bill for the excess, unless you have private insurance.

General Tax Considerations

If you know that your income is going to drop dramatically in the current tax year, you may want to request a "Waiver of Deduction at Source" from Revenue Canada. This may come in handy if, for example, it is early in the year and you are planning to return to school in September. If Revenue Canada grants a waiver, some or all of the tax deducted from your paycheque will be reduced. In order to request such a waiver you should contact your local Revenue Canada office.

If you are planning a leave for the birth or adoption of your first child, keep in mind that a whole set of tax arrangements will come into place with a new dependant in the household. You or your spouse will be able to claim a dependant deduction for the child, and you may be eligible for a child tax credit.

If you are taking a leave of absence to return to school, you should remember that you will become eligible for the tuition deduction in 1987 and the education tax credit starting in 1988.

If you know that you will be earning much lower income in some year before 1997, you may want to investigate the forward-averaging provision in your 1987 tax return. Forward averaging gives people a federal tax credit that can be used in a future year of extraordinarily low income. In order to make use of it, you will need to have earned relatively high income in 1987 to claim the credit. Forward averaging credits will not be able to be claimed after 1987 if scheduled White Paper reforms go into place. The White Paper has also scheduled 1997 as the last year in which the credits will be able to be used in a year of low income.

PART-TIME WORK AND JOB SHARING

While the rapid recent growth in part-time work is not expected to continue through to the end of this century, the Commission of Inquiry into Part-time Work — a major study of the topic done for the federal Minister of Labour in 1983 — predicts that it still will be attractive to growing numbers of people. The report of the Commission stated, "there will be a continuing increase in the supply of people who prefer to work part-time — not always as a permanent choice, but at various periods in their lives."

Getting a Part-Time Job

While switching from full-time to part-time status may be difficult, it is not always impossible. If you have developed specialized knowledge required by your employer, or if you are needed to fill particular production shifts, your employer will likely be opposed to any request for part-time work. But employers in particular industries are accustomed to dealing with part-time workers. You stand a better chance of getting part-time work if you apply to employers in those industries.

According to figures cited in the Commission of Inquiry into Part-time Work, the largest employers of part-time workers are retail stores, with part-timers working in sales, office, clerical, data processing, warehousing and delivery jobs. The tourism, hotel and food-service industry also employs large numbers of part-time workers. But there are also significant opportunities for part-time work in health care, banking and insurance, manufacturing, municipal government and transportation services.

Job Sharing

The Commission of Inquiry into Part-time Work defined job sharing as "a voluntary arrangement between two individuals (or in rare occasions more than two) and their employer to enable the employees to share what are normally the duties of one full-time person." Employees working in job-sharing arrangements are usually paid wages and benefits that are prorated to full-time wages and benefits.

Most job sharers work in professional and clerical occupations in hospital and other health services, education, social work and office work. The most common kinds of job-sharing arrangements are: 1) one person works Monday, Tuesday and every second Wednesday, while the other works Thursday, Friday and every other Wednesday; and 2) the partners work half-weeks, split at noon on Wednesday. Not all job partners share exactly the same responsibilities. Some partners have separate responsibilities, even though they are theoretically splitting the same job.

According to the Commission's report, several employers said that job sharing is most successful when it is requested by the employees themselves, and when the two individuals are very compatible. The report also said that many of the job sharers suggested that they had to work extra hard to prove to their employers that the concept could succeed.

If you want to explore the possiblity of job sharing, you should consider the following checklist of issues, as suggested by the Commission:

- Seniority. Ensure that seniority provisions are discussed and agreed to by the job sharers and employer. Will seniority accumulate in terms of hours, or half-years? This will affect both pension and layoff provisions.
- Salary increments. Will salary raises be granted according to regular yearly advances, or will job sharers have to put in an equivalent number of "person-weeks" to advance to a higher rate of pay?
- Future return to a full-time position. You should have a pre-arranged agreement for return to full-time work. Do you have a right to a full-time job after a specified period? Do you have a right to a full-time job when one comes available? Or must you compete with other applicants for any available openings?
- What if one partner leaves? Will the employer continue to keep the job-sharing arrangement? What say does the remaining partner have in choosing the successor? How will the opening be covered until a replacement is found?
- Overtime. If the partners are scheduled to work twenty hours a week, is overtime paid if more than twenty hours is worked by either partner?
- Extra "On call" hours. To what extent and on what occasions are the partners required to work more than twenty hours a week?
- Splitting benefits. How do job sharers — who work part-time — participate in full-time benefits?
- Career advancement. Will a job-sharing arrangement jeopardize the career advancement prospects of the partners? Will there be opportunities for in-service training and upgrading programs?

- Communication procedures. Communication procedures between partners and with supervisors should be formalized and understood before the arrangement starts.

Tax Considerations

Needless to say, there is much less income from a part-time job or a job-sharing position than from a full-time job. However, if you are making the calculation about whether to drop down to part-time work, you should not forget that important tax benefits may accrue from lower taxable income. While these benefits will not totally compensate you for your thinner wallet, they might make the bite a little easier to take.

Perhaps most important, you should remember that your marginal tax rate could drop if your income drops. For example, in 1988 and subsequent years, if your taxable income is about $28,000, it will not take much of an income drop to cut your federal/provincial marginal tax rate from about 39 per cent to 25.5 per cent. You will be earning less money, certainly, but you will also be required to pay less tax.

As discussed in chapter 4, there are also a number of basic personal tax exemptions that you can claim in 1987. In 1988, these are scheduled to be converted into tax credits. The married and equivalent-to-married exemptions or credits are available to your spouse only if you earn less than a specified total. These exemptions or credits are significant if you earn very little money, but some low-income part-timers might qualify.

For example, in 1987, if you will earn less than $520, your spouse can claim a married exemption of $3,700 against his or her income. If you will earn more than $520, your spouse can deduct $4,220 minus your income. The equivalent-to-married deduction — available to single mothers, among other people — also amounts to $3,700 if you earn less than $520, or $4,220 minus whatever income over $520.

In 1988, if you will earn less than $500, your spouse will be able to claim a married tax credit of about $1,315. This credit will be reduced by 17 per cent of your net income in excess of $500. The equivalent to married tax credit will operate in the same way.

EARLY RETIREMENT

A growing number of people are considering work beyond the traditional retirement age of sixty-five. But there are also large numbers of employees who are considering an early retirement. If you are one of these, you must weigh a number of financial factors, including government benefits, pension plans, annuity or RRIF income, and your tax situation. Fortunately for early retirees, federal and provincial governments have been loosening pension and RRSP rules in the last few years to make early retirement easier.

Canada Pension Plan/Quebec Pension Plan

People who are at least sixty-five are eligible for three basic types of government income — the Canada Pension Plan/Quebec Pension Plan (CPP/QPP), the Old Age Security (OAS) and the Guaranteed Income Supplement (GIS). The OAS is the basic federal old-age pension eligible to all Canadians who have reached sixty-five and meet certain residency requirements. GIS supplements the income of needy people who are at least sixty-five. Unless you are a very-low-income earner, you will not be eligible to receive the GIS. Since OAS and GIS begin after age sixty-five, they will not be discussed in detail here. However, if you are considering early retirement, and you are worried about your income after age sixty-five, you should try to make an estimate of what your post-sixty-five income will be, once the OAS is added.

The government program that can begin before age sixty-five is the CPP or, in Quebec, the QPP. People are eligible to receive a CPP pension if they are at least sixty and have contributed to the plan at some point since it was established in 1966.

An important point for people who are considering early retirement is that, if you are between sixty and sixty-four, CPP requires that you must have "wholly or substantially ceased working." This means that you must have employment earnings that are less than the maximum CPP pension receivable at age sixty-five. In 1987, this was $521.52 a month. Once you qualify you can continue to receive your pension even if your income increases above the limit.

Different retirees have different CPP pensions, which will vary by the number of years you have contributed, your average wages in your contribution period and whether you had any unusual low-income periods.

People who are considering an early retirement should ask CPP to provide an estimate of their retirement pension because they will receive a lower payment than they would if they waited until sixty-five or later to begin receiving the pension. CPP will reduce your pension by 0.5 per cent for every month (or 6 per cent a year) you begin receiving benefits before age sixty-five and will increase it by 0.5 per cent for every month after sixty-five to seventy.

This can make a big difference in your income. For example, if you are eligible for the maximum CPP pension, but you begin drawing it at age sixty, you receive only $364 a month instead of the $521.52 (according to the maximum 1987 payout) you would receive if you had waited until age sixty-five. Since CPP does not readjust your pension at age sixty-five, you are stuck with that pension for the rest of your life. The only change that will be made is an adjustment to reflect changes in the Consumer Price Index, the government's measure of inflation.

Employer Pensions

About 40 per cent of Canadians in the labour force are members of employer pension plans. Since these plans vary widely, it is best to check with your employer about specific early retirement benefits.

Under recent federal and Ontario pension-reform legislation, people who want to retire early from their jobs will be able to receive pensions from their employer plans as early as ten years before the normal retirement age. For most plans, this means that employees will be able to start collecting at age fifty-five.

Other provinces are following suit in this sort of legislation. To determine whether or not you are eligible for early retirement benefits, ask your employer.

RRIF/Annuity Provisions

As mentioned in chapter 2, people who have reached the age of seventy-one are required to collapse their RRSP, or roll it over into a registered retirement income fund (RRIF) or annuity. The RRIF or annuity distributes the proceeds of the RRSP in retirement years. Under new rules introduced in the February 1986 budget, people may make use of any of these provisions at any time before they are seventy-one. This means that people considering early retirement can make use of these post-RRSP products even though they may still have many years before they turn seventy-one and even if they have not yet turned sixty-five.

To decide whether you want to make use of the post-RRSP products or simply withdraw money from your RRSP you will need a sharp pencil, thorough consultations with RRIF and annuity sales representatives, and a bit of financial forecasting. As a rule of thumb, if you expect inflation to rise, you should probably avoid annuities because rising prices will erode the value of your annuity income. Keeping your RRSP investments intact or in an RRIF will give you the option of moving them into higher-income investments if inflation turns upward.

As already indicated, RRIFs and RRSPs are superior to annuities for investors who want to retain control over the ethical use of their funds.

Pension Income Tax Deduction

People receiving eligible pension income are entitled to a deduction of up to $1,000 for 1987. The White Paper on tax reform suggests changing this in 1988 and subsequent years to a tax credit of 17 per cent of eligible pension income, up to a maximum credit of $170.

If you are sixty-five or older, you may claim the deduction for a wide variety of types of pension income. These include payments from a pension plan, RRIF or annuity. If you are under sixty-five, the only kind of pension income you will be able to claim for deduction is payment from a pension plan. (Special rules affect people who are receiving a disability or survivor's pension).

6

RESOURCES — GETTING HELP OR DOING IT YOURSELF

Finding a stock broker or financial adviser who appreciates the problems of ethical money management can be a frustrating, time-consuming task. The recent experience of a Toronto woman is, unfortunately, all too typical.

The woman — a novice investor — was contacted by a representative from a major Bay Street firm when he telephoned everyone in her office looking for RRSP business. His firm had a contest for brokers who could sign up the largest number of new accounts. At their first meeting, they started talking stocks.

She told the representative right from the start that she was not interested in companies like Litton Systems — the missile-guidance-equipment manufacturer. Instead, she said, she would be interested in some of the ethical funds that she had heard about.

The stock broker was surprised. "Oh, no one's ever asked me about those before," he said. "Do you mind if I look for the one that has the best rate of return?"

Unfortunately, all too many brokers among Bay Street investment firms are woefully ignorant of the aims of ethical investors. Ethical investing appears as a peculiar endeavour to many brokers. Trained in Canadian Securities Institute courses emphasizing financial ratios, tax accounting and the business cycle, they are intellectually unprepared for the application of values to investments. In the pressure-cooker world of the stock markets, the world of ethics and ideas seems unreal when set against the money to be made by stock transactions.

Even if a broker is sympathetic, he or she may be handicapped by a lack of knowledge of the ethical history of his or her favourite stock choices. Full-service stock brokerage companies have research departments, and stock analysts are sensitive to social concerns that may affect stock prices, but the application of ethical criteria to stocks is foreign to most of these people.

Financial planners who analyse your overall economic situation may also be in a blatant conflict of interest if at the same time they earn their income from commissions by selling insurance policies, mutual funds or other financial products.

But take heart. It may take some work, but there are ways to find financial advisers sympathetic to your concerns. The Canadian Network for Ethical Investment can provide a list of its members who have agreed to include their names on a "networking" list. The list includes names of investment professionals who can help you in your financial decision-making. This chapter gives other suggestions for finding advisers.

You may also want to step cautiously into the investment waters yourself by researching and purchasing ethical investments on your own. Some of the information costs a few dollars; other information can cost thousands. Fortunately, however, much of this information is free and may be obtained easily from your public library.

FINANCIAL ADVISERS

Financial Planners

A financial planner is an adviser who will gather information on your assets, liabilities and income, ask you how you feel about risk and return, analyse this information in terms of your goals, age and family situation, and present financial strategies to help you reach your goals. A financial planner sensitive to ethical money management will also determine your priorities and suggest strategies to reach your financial goals while staying consistent with your social criteria.

Some financial planners provide advice for a fee and do not offer any financial products for sale, some give free planning advice and are paid on commissions of products sold, while others charge fees for specific financial advice and also receive product commissions. A good number of the firms listed in the financial planning consultants section of your local Yellow Pages are sales representatives for insurance companies and mutual funds.

"Most financial planners are in a conflict-of-interest situation because they mix advice to consumers with the selling of products and thus have an incentive to advise customers to invest in the products they are selling," warns *A Framework for Financial Regulation*, a 1987 report prepared for the Economic Council of Canada. "It is not always clear that consumers are fully aware of the existence of such a conflict of interest."

Therefore, it is important to ask a prospective planner how he or she is paid. Planners who work on a commission basis may not necessarily be the worst option for consumers, because they may be able to provide good advice at low cost (fee-for-service planners charge between $50 and $200 an hour, and a full-blown analysis can cost as much as $5,000). But if you choose a planner paid from commissions you will want to satisfy yourself that all your financial options are being considered. If you choose a fee-for-service planner, you will want to satisfy yourself that you are getting value for your money.

You will also want to ask your financial planner whether he or she has a Chartered Financial Planner (CFP) designation from the Canadian Institute of Financial Planning. In order to receive a CFP designation, a planner must complete six special courses and have at least two years of work experience in financial planning.

The Canadian Association of Financial Planners (address in appendix 3) has information on selecting a financial planner. You can obtain a list of planners in your area who are members of the association.

From an ethical point of view, you may also want to ask your planner whether he or she is a member of the Canadian Network for Ethical Investment and has some familiarity with the ethical investment movement. In addition, you may want to know whether he or she sells any of the ethical mutual funds.

Stock Brokers

Stock brokers are agents who act on behalf of buyers or sellers of stock to execute their transactions. Individuals who perform this function are known as registered representatives (RRs) and are licensed by provincial securities commissions.

While the stock broker title gives the impression that these people deal only in stock-market securities, most brokerage firms deal in a variety of investments, including stocks, bonds and debentures.

Stock brokers are paid on a commission charged for the buying or selling of investments. So-called full-service brokers provide research, advisory and stock-trading services, while discount brokerage firms offer trading-services only.

The Canadian Securities Institute recommends that the best way to choose a broker is on the recommendation of a friend, acquaintance, business associate or professional who has already received satisfactory service. Investors can also obtain a list of major securities companies by writing to the Investment Dealers Association of Canada (address in appendix 3), which includes all major stock-brokerage companies.

Ethical investing is advancing slowly in the Canadian securities industry, but it may be possible to ask the major brokerage firms whether or not any of their registered representatives are ethical investment specialists.

Credit Unions

Many credit unions across the country are also offering personal financial planning advice for their members. Some — the Ottawa Womens' Credit Union is one — charge on an hourly basis for members to meet with financial professionals, such as accountants. Other credit unions, such as DUCA Credit Union in Toronto, offer counselling sessions or special courses, which are free of charge to members. These sessions are scheduled at particular times of the year — usually at year-end or in January or February — to attract members interested in RRSP or tax planning.

Investment Counsellors, Lawyers and Accountants

These advisers are generally for investors who have a great deal of money to invest, or special financial-planning problems. Accountants can be used to fill out your income-tax form or to provide financial advice. There is no rule of thumb for determining who needs an accountant. Generally, however, financial planners advise self-employed people or anyone earning more than $50,000 a year to consider using an accountant. Accountants' fees range between $50 and $250 an hour.

Lawyers can be used to look after the legal aspects of your financial planning, and the drafting of documents such as wills, trusts, business contracts, and divorce and separation settlements. Most investors probably do not require the services of a lawyer, but some specialized ethical investors might need legal advice. If you choose to invest RRSP money in a private company, for example, or preferred shares in a cooperative, it might be best to have a lawyer draft or review the investment agreement.

Investment counsellors are generally only for the most well-heeled investor. They manage investment portfolios on behalf of investors who generally have at least $50,000 to invest. They generally charge a flat fee of about 1 per cent of investments and will sometimes go to bat for clients at securities commissions on behalf of clients who have been wronged by majority-shareholder actions or other securities infractions.

DOING IT YOURSELF

Choosing a mutual fund, picking stocks or finding community-based investments on your own takes some work, but it can be a real learning experience. What is more, it can be fun. This kind of research combines all the enjoyment of detective work with the thrill of playing with investments. It also holds the possibility of helping you to develop a deeper understanding of our society, and the ways in which business meets or dodges its corporate responsibilities.

Mutual Funds

The information you need most on mutual funds concerns the ethical criteria of the various funds, as well as their short- and long-term performance. The appendix in this book carries a list of the ethical mutual funds operating at the time of writing (1987), but you should write to the Canadian Network for Ethical Investment for an up-to-date list.

Once you have narrowed down a list of possible investment funds, you are well advised to write to the various funds for prospectuses. A prospectus is a legal document filed by any mutual fund offered to the public. Prospectuses must be filed with provincial securities commissions, and must contain up-to-date financial information.

As mentioned in the chapter on investment, daily newspapers carry listings of the unit values of investment funds. The *Financial Post* and the *Financial Times of Canada*, Canada's two leading financial newspapers, publish regular listings that provide more detailed information.

One of the pieces of information that is most important to consider is the annual compounded rate of return. This figure allows you to compare the return of various funds on a basis of one year, three years, five years, or even longer. While a high one-year return may sound tempting, it is important to look at the longer-term performance of a fund.

You should also compare mutual-fund performance with the performance of general stock-market indicators, such as the TSE 300 Index in Canada and the Standard and Poor's 500 Index in the United States.

You might also want to review measures that give an indication of whether the performance of your fund has been fairly constant over time, or whether your fund has been hit by big peaks and valleys. These are called variability estimates or reward-risk ratios. If unit values have risen and plunged sharply in the last year, this shows that your fund contains high-risk stocks. Most investors will want a fund that demonstrates a good return over time, with little variability.

The basic question is: What is a good return? As rule of thumb, you will want your mutual fund to exceed other stock market measures like the TSE 300. You will also want the performance of your fund to approach the average performance of other, similar funds.

Researching Stocks

One place that novice ethical investors can look for stocks is the portfolio lists of the ethical funds. (Lists for some of these funds are included in appendix 5).

You should write to these funds for an up-to-date prospectus, which will include a list of current holdings. By investigating this list, and placing at least a portion of your portfolio in one of these funds, you can get a feel for the kinds of companies that are currently favoured by investment professionals screening companies for social and financial performance. Since there are often dozens of companies included in a mutual fund portfolio, it will take a little work to narrow down these lists to the short list that will actually make up your investment portfolio.

At the outset, you can narrow your list to companies in industries with which you are ethically comfortable. If you are concerned about the sustainablility of non-renewable resources, for instance, you will not want to invest in energy, forestry or mining companies, even if they have a good record on employee relations or South Africa.

You should also choose industries that show economic promise. Many high-technology companies have produced nothing but losses for their shareholders, but many have also been big winners because of office automation and other technological trends. Technology companies appeal to many ethical investors because they generally have good environmental records.

At this stage you will want to research individual companies. You can often obtain an annual report by calling or writing to the local or head offices of these companies. Companies are keen to distribute their annual reports, and will provide one free of charge.

The annual report contains essential financial information (more on this later), along with clues to its ethical record. Some of the things you will want to look for in the report include a code of conduct, a list of charitable contributions, a mention of special programs for employees, the list of directors (Are there women on the board?), environmental programs (if the company has a history of environmental problems) and any lawsuits or other legal action against the company.

At this point, you may want to do further ethical research. Libraries carry news indices that often contain references to news-stories on major companies. Many libraries also carry detailed corporate information, such as *The Financial Post Survey of Industrials*. This survey will give you a detailed breakdown of the affiliates and subsidiaries of major Canadian corporations. You can use this information to see whether your companies are connected with other companies with poor social records.

You may also want to ask for reports from various organizations conducting research on special issues. The Taskforce on the Churches and Corporate Responsibility (TCCR) deals with companies on a number of social issues. The SACTU (South African Congress of Trade Unions) Solidarity Committee (Canada) provides extensive information on business links with South Africa. The Canadian Labour Congress can provide information on companies under a union boycott. And Greenpeace Canada can give you information on companies with environmental problems. (Addresses are in appendix 3).

On military issues, you should check the book *Arms Canada* by Ernie Regehr, research director of Project Ploughshares. Published by James Lorimer & Company in 1987, the book provides a detailed list of companies involved in military production.

Another book, *The Financial Post Selects the 100 Best Companies to Work for in Canada*, published by Totem, gives a list of companies with positive labour practices. However, the list should be treated with caution by investors concerned about the trade union record of companies because there are many companies included in the book that have been criticized by unions trying to organize them.

If you want a definitive ethical check on your companies, you can ask Ethicscan Canada, which bills itself as a clearinghouse for consumer and corporate ethics, to provide corporate profiles. Ethicscan will prepare reports on selected companies on a wide variety of ethical issues. The cost of the reports is about $100 per company. If you deal with a stock broker, you may get Ethicscan information through your broker's company, if the company has a contract with Ethicscan to supply profiles. Ethicscan also has plans to issue newsletters on various issues concerning corporate responsibility. (Address in appendix 3).

In terms of financial information, the annual reports of the companies on your short list will provide four main pieces of essential data. These are: the earnings statement (what revenue was taken in, what expenses were paid out and how much profit was left), the balance sheet of assets (what the company owns) and liabilities (what it owes), the changes of financial position (how the cash flowing in and out of the company was employed in the last few years) and the statement of retained earnings (how much profit was distributed to the shareholders and how much was retained for use by the company). These statements should be examined carefully to determine whether the company has been earning steady profits over the last few years and whether its balance sheet is deteriorating, improving or staying the same.

You should also begin following the business press for earnings announcements and other corporate developments concerning your companies. The *Globe and Mail Report on Business* is the most widely recommended source. The financial newspapers also carry regular stories on individual companies. Many libraries carry the magazine *Investors Digest*, which carries investment reviews by leading financial analysts.

You may also want to contact the Canadian Securities Institute (address in appendix 3), which publishes the guidebook *How to Invest in Canadian Securities*. The institute offers home-study courses and more advanced courses for investment professionals and ordinary investors.

The Canadian Securities Institute material explains such things as the fundamental economic factors motivating the stock market and technical ratios you can use to analyse the performance of your companies.

Once you choose a particular company in which to invest, you will have to choose whether or not you want to purchase common stock, preferred shares, bonds, debentures or more sophisticated investments such as rights, warrants and options. In most cases, you will want to purchase common or preferred shares. Guides such as *The Financial Post Survey of Industrials* lists the types of investments available. (See the earlier chapter on investment for a discussion of the various kinds of investments).

Purchasing Stocks

Once you have satisfied yourself of the financial and ethical soundness of of your stock choices, the time has come to make the purchase.

The first decision is whether to use RRSP/RRIF or money outside such plans for the purchase. If you are using RRSP or RRIF money, you will have to open a self-directed plan in order to trade in stocks. Trust companies, securities dealers and many banks offer self-directed RRSPs and RRIFs.

The second decision you will have to make is whether to purchase your stock through a full-commission broker or through a discount broker. The traditional way of trading in stock was through full- service securities dealers, who employ brokers, research analysts and a trading team that buys and sells shares. With such a large staff, brokerage fees have traditionally been quite hefty.

Traditional Toronto Stock Exchange fees — fixed by the TSE — were 3 per cent on shares less than $5, 2 per cent plus five cents a share on stock valued at between $5 and $15, and 1 per cent plus 20 cents a share on shares valued at more than $15. However, in 1983 the Montreal and Toronto exchanges abolished fixed rates, and now there are a number of discount brokers who charge rates significantly below the traditional fees. The full-service brokers now generally charge commissions higher than the traditional rates. The discount firms are able to charge less because they do not offer services such as research reports and personal service to clients. But, for investors who know what they want to buy or sell, the discount brokers provide the best deal.

The securities industry estimates that discount brokerage firms handle less than 10 per cent of the securities transaction business, but their share of the market is growing. Several of the large banks offer discount brokerage services, along with a few securities dealers, such as Marathon Brown, Gardiner Group and Disnat Investment. The discounts offered by these firms can be subtantial. For example, one discount broker charges $60 for a trade of 1,000 shares at $3.95 a share, while a full-commission broker would charge $129.13. In this case, a discount broker would save the investor $69 — 54 per cent — on an investment of $3,950.

In order to open a discount brokerage account, you will have to visit or telephone a branch of a discount trading firm. A representative of the firm will send you an application for a discount trading account. You can keep cash or other investments in this account until you wish to trade in stock. Many of the institutions will take trading orders over the telephone.

Shares are usually purchased in multiples of 100. To buy shares, you will have to decide what kind of order you wish to give. Two of the most common types of orders are market orders, issued to purchase shares at the best available price, and limit orders, which specify that shares cannot be bought or sold above or below a certain price.

Credit Unions and Alternative Investments

The best way to find a credit union in your community is to write or telelphone the Canadian Co-operative Credit Society, the national financial institution for credit unions, or provincial credit-union centrals (addresses in appendix 1). They can provide a list of credit unions operating in your area. When you contact these organizations you should also mention whether you wish to belong to an ethnic, union or other closed-bond credit union, or whether you prefer a community or open-bond credit union. The majority of credit unions in provinces outside Ontario have open bonds.

Alternative investments are more difficult to track down than mutual funds and corporate investments, but there are a few organizations across the country that can put you in touch with needy enterprises.

A list of community loan funds and other types of alternative investments is included in appendix 8. For direct investments in cooperative or alternative enterprises, investors should contact one of a number of consultancy organizations that do research for this kind of business.

Three of these are Co-op Work in Toronto, Working Margins Consultants in Winnipeg, and Westcoast Research and Information Cooperative, which has offices in Vancouver and other cities in British Columbia. (Adresses in appendix 3).

You will also be able to find information about innovative economic programs in your area by contacting the Canadian Jobs Strategy, a program of the federal Department of Employment and Immigration (address in appendix 3). CJS sponsors local community employment initiatives that sometimes require local investment.

CONCLUSION

On March 17, 1987, a little-noticed but remarkable event happened on the Toronto Stock Exchange. After International Thomson Organisation Ltd. — the newspaper, oil and retailing giant — announced the sale of its South African subsidiary, the company's stock *climbed* 25 cents a share. At just under $15, the result was the stock's highest price in at least a year.

The event was a sign of the times on Bay Street. Gone are the days when Canadian corporations would flock to South Africa in search of high-grade mineral deposits, an expanding industrial market and cheap labour-force. Although the number of Canadian companies operating in South Africa climbed from twenty-eight in 1981 to thirty-five a year later, by the spring of 1987 the total was down to less than a dozen.

Companies such as Alcan Aluminium Ltd. originally balked at withdrawing from South Africa. But after church groups promised to bring the issue to the floor of Alcan's annual meeting in 1986, the company sold its interest in a South African aluminum producer. As Bill Davis, financial secretary for the United Church, said in congratulating Alcan "good corporate citizenship and sound business judgement are compatible. The company's decision to sell can be seen as one further signal to the government of South Africa that its apartheid policy does not sit well on any grounds, moral or business."

Feisty shareholder activists, environmentalists, peace groups, consumer advocates and unionists are joining with ethical investors to usher in a new approach to business. This new approach appreciates that there are more "stakeholders" in a corporation than just the shareholders who legally own the company and the managers who run it. Employees — many of whom have invested decades of labour and know-how — have a stake. Communities that provide roads to transport corporate goods and schools to educate corporate workforces also have a legitimate stake in the corporation. Even society as a whole has a stake when corporate actions threaten the environment or the economic well-being of the public.

Traditional managements take a different attitude. They maintain that the only group to which they have an obligation is the shareholders — the group that legally and formally owns the company. This means that the only responsibility the managers have is to ensure that share prices keep rising and dividends keep getting fatter.

With ethically minded people flocking into capital markets, it is investors themselves who are beginning to challenge this view. Ethical investors now demand that corporations look to more than rising profits. In response to their pressure, many corporate managements now believe that they must be good corporate citizens in order to keep their share prices high and profits growing.

REAL CHANGE OR CLEVER PR?

Undoubtedly, many corporations are feeling the heat and changing their public images. Corporate codes of conduct are more common now than they were only a few years ago. Many corporations are adopting pollution standards that are tougher than government regulations require. Others are working to involve their employees in the decision-making process. And while corporate donations to charities are still well below the 1-per-cent level of pre-tax profit contributed in the 1960s, more companies are opening their coffers to charities.

University of Toronto business professor Leonard Brooks, writing in the groundbreaking book *Canadian Corporate Social Performance*, found that major Canadian corporations are facing far higher expectations for *social* performance in 1985 than they did in 1980, 1975 or 1970.

> Already a sizeable portion of Canadian executives believe in corporate social performance, and as more and more executives, union leaders and politicians come to share this belief, significant reluctance to pursue corporate social performance goals will be overcome. If so, the integration of economic and social goals, which is at the root of corporate social performance, could become widespread by 1990.

But how much of all this represents real concern for corporate stakeholders, and how much of it reflects mere motherhood issues that are easy to support and cost little? Take the Canadian tobacco industry, for example.

The industry has been under economic pressure for years, battling a decline in cigarette consumption. The public now widely accepts cigarette smoking as a health hazard, and governments have gradually been reducing the right of the industry to advertise. In 1987, the federal government introduced legislation to ban all cigarette advertising by 1989. As the industry's public image has sunk, it has spent more money to persuade the public and political leaders that it really is a good corporate citizen.

Imasco Ltd., for example, which owns Imperial Tobacco — the largest tobacco company in Canada — spent nearly $2 million in fiscal 1987 in donations to five hundred Canadian charities. In addition, the company has committed $7 million to the Montreal Job Creation Initiative, which will assist entrepreneurs in establishing new businesses. In its 1987 annual report, Imasco said it chose Montreal because of the historic connection between the city and Imperial Tobacco, which has its head office located there.

Undoubtedly these projects reflect a commitment to good corporate citizenship. But they also reflect a desire to improve the image of the tobacco industry. Imperial sponsors golf and tennis tournaments, equestrian events, motor races and the Royal Winnipeg Ballet. The company wants consumers to attach a healthful, athletic and artsy image to its product.

As far as ethical investors are concerned, it does not really matter what motivates companies to do good works. Still, they should recognize that companies may trip over themselves to carry out good works — especially if they are restricted in advertising — to improve a poor image. For ethical investors, the fundamental image problem may be a good reason to avoid a company, however socially responsible its behaviour may be.

While the ethical investment movement can claim some credit for advances on many issues — particularly South Africa — ethical investors should not become complacent. It is important to do more than simply screen your investments — you must ensure that your voice is heard. This means monitoring the social performance of the investments you choose, and making sure that corporate executives hear from you if they do something of which you disapprove.

UNLEASHING CAPITAL

If the Canadian Network for Ethical Investment is right, there could be millions, perhaps billions, of dollars that will eventually be defined as ethical investment in Canada. "The pension funds of unions, university faculty associations and churches (just to mention those which are likely to move first) hold hundreds of millions of dollars," the network said in its Summer 1987 newsletter. "Very few of these organizations are presently applying social criteria to their investments in spite of the fact that such a move would be in harmony with the purposes and the principles of the organizations."

These millions, while representing a small proportion of the funds in Canadian capital markets, could act as a vanguard for social change. Not only could they help to bolster the share prices of responsible corporations, and make it easier for those corporations to raise capital, but they could help to fund new enterprises that are sensitive to human needs and create jobs in economically distressed regions.

The union movement, for example, is waking up to the fact that it holds tremendous power through union-sponsored pension funds. Union members are becoming tired of companies skimming employee funds or investing the funds in reprehensible investments. "If we can't solve that problem through the legislative process then we'll damn well go to the bargaining table with it," Gord Wilson, newly-chosen president of the Ontario Federation of Labour, told the OFL convention in 1986. "Why shouldn't we think of taking control of pension funds as trade unions and using the money for socially useful purposes?"

This kind of agressive, future-looking investment is not the kind of investment that has traditionally been served up by Canadian banks, insurance companies, trust firms and securities dealers. Since the fur trade established the economic foundation of this country, Canadian financial institutions have poured money into huge resource projects; but they have poured relatively little into manufacturing and other job-intensive industries. British and American multinationals filled this void, establishing fragmented and inefficient manufacturing plants. Fed by the Canadian compulsion to save, Canadian financial institutions fulfilled Canada's destiny as an underdeveloped society dependent on natural resources.

While the assets of ethical investors may never reach the size of the huge funds controlled by conventional financial institutions, the movement has the potential to help develop a new kind of Canadian economy. Because ethical investment is sensitive to social requirements, it can nurture enterprises that meet local needs rather than the business demands of international corporations. It can also encourage greater democracy in our economic institutions by giving people a say in business decisions if those decisions affect them as consumers, employees, residents or citizens.

The ethical investment movement represents one of the ways in which ordinary Canadians can collectively take control of their financial future.

APPENDICES

APPENDIX 1

Central Organizations for Credit Unions, *Caisses Populaires,* **and Cooperative Trust and Insurance Companies**

Credit-Union Centrals

Canadian Co-operative Credit Society
    300 The East Mall
    5th Floor
    Islington, Ont.
    M9B 6B7

British Columbia Central Credit Union
    1441 Creekside Drive
    Vancouver, B.C.
    V6J 4S7

Credit Union Central of Alberta
    #350 — 8500 Macleod Trail S.E.
    Calgary, Alta.
    T2H 2N1

Credit Union Central of Saskatchewan
    P.O. Box 3030
    Regina, Sask.
    S4P 3G8

Credit Union Central of Manitoba
    P.O. Box 9900
    Winnipeg, Man.
    R3C 3E2

Credit Union Central of Ontario
    180 Duncan Mill Road
    Don Mills, Ont.
    M3B 3K3

Confédération des caisses populaires
   et d'économie Desjardins du Québec
   100 av. des Commandeurs
   Lévis, Quebec.
   G6V 7N5

Credit Union Central of Nova Scotia
   P.O. Box 9200
   Station A
   Halifax, N.S.
   B3K 5N3

Credit Union Central of Prince Edward Island
   P.O. Box 968
   Charlottetown, P.E.I.
   C1A 7M4

Credit Union Central of New Brunswick
   P.O. Box 1025
   Moncton, N.B.
   E1C 8P2

Credit Union Council of Newfoundland
   P.O. Box 13004
   Postal Station A
   19 Crosbie Place
   St. John's, Nfld.
   A1B 3V8

Insurance

The Co-operators Group Ltd.
   Priory Square
   Guelph, Ont.
   N1H 6P8

CUMIS Life Insurance Co.
   P.O. Box 5065
   Burlington, Ont.
   L7R 9Z9

Trust

Co-operative Trust Co. of Canada
    333 — 3rd Avenue North
    Saskatoon, Sask.
    S7K 2M2

League Savings and Mortgage
    P.O. Box 8900
    6074 Lady Hammond Road
    Halifax, N.S.
    B3K 5M5

APPENDIX 2

Guidelines of the Committee on Social Responsibility in Investment, Presbyterian Church in Canada[1]

Category 1

The social responsibility of companies concerning the rights and needs of their employees.
- Wages of employees: Does the company pay adequate wages and benefits required for a decent human life? How do the company's wages and fringe benefits compare with other companies, other regions? How do percentage wage increases compare with percentage increases in profits?
- Working conditions: Does the company provide safeguards for the health and safety of its employees? How do these safeguards compare with those of similar companies? Are there any provisions for job security for the company's employees?
- Trade unions: Does the company accept the rights of the employees to organize through trade unions? What has been the company's relationship with trade unions in the past?

[1]For further information, contact: Committee on Social Responsibility in Investment Policy, Presbyterian Church in Canada, c/o Secretary, 50 Wynford Dr., Don Mills, Ont., M3C 1J7.

• Employee participation: Does the company involve employees effectively in its decision-making process? Is the company open to forms of worker ownership or worker control?

Category 2

The social responsibility of companies concerning the economic development of the community or country in which they operate.

• Underdeveloped regions: Does the company have operations in relatively poor underdeveloped communities or regions? What impact does the company have in improving the economic conditions of the community?

• Job creation: Does the company provide a large number of permanent jobs for the people of the community? Are the company's operations primarily labour-intensive or capital- intensive?

• Resource extraction: Is the community involved in processing and manufacturing its own resources? Does the company effectively limit the community's development to that of supplying raw materials?

• Tax incentives: Does the company require tax incentives from governments as conditions for investment? What impact does this have on the long-term economic development of the community?

• Capital reinvestment: Does the company reinvest its profits in the community to serve local development needs, or are these profits taken out of the community for investment elsewhere?

Category 3

The social responsibility of companies concerning the social and environmental conditions of the community or country in which they operate.

• Company towns: Does the company operate company towns or one-industry communities? What kind of control does it exercise over credit, police, products, laws, trade unions, cultural and educational activities?

• Land use: Does the company own or control large tracts of agricultural land? Is the land being used adequately for food production?

- Internal migration: Do the company's operations compel workers to leave their land and migrate from rural to urban centres? What impact does this have on family life in the region?
- Minority groups: Does the company have a policy of providing jobs for minority groups in the labour force? Are the language, customs and values of minority groups respected by the company?
- Pollution problems: Does the company use technology that causes pollution of air, water or other forms of environmental damage?

Category 4

The social responsibility of companies concerning the civil, political and religious liberties of the community or country in which they operate.

- Repressive régimes: Does the company have operations in countries based on separation and subordination of certain races? Do the company's operations effectively support or oppose racial apartheid in these situations?
- Religious freedom: Does the company have operations in countries or regions where there are state restrictions on religious freedom? Does the company actively support or oppose these conditions?
- Cheap labour: Does the company have operations in countries or regions where trade unions are outlawed or restricted in their activities? Does the company take advantage of the cheap labour conditions?

Category 5

The social responsibility of companies concerning production and marketing of their products.

- Consumer goods: Does the company produce and sell luxury goods or basic necessities required by the majority of people? Is the company's product designed to meet consumer needs and to be durable and long-lasting?
- Harmful products: Does the company produce and/or sell products which are harmful or destructive of human life?
- Arms production: Does the company engage in any aspect of arms production?

- Advertising practices: Does the company's advertising present a true rather than a false or misleading description of their products? Does the company's advertising refrain from any form of discrimination or exploitation of particular groups (racial minorities, women, etc.)? Is advertising used to create artificial needs?
- Monopoly control: Does the company exercise monopoly control over its particular markets, either by itself or as a subsidiary of another corporation? Has the company had a record of unfair business practices, trust or monopoly violations, or price fixing?

APPENDIX 3

Resource Organizations and Publications

Ethical Investment Information

Canadian Labour Congress
    2841 Riverside Drive
    Ottawa, Ont.
    T1V 8X7

Provides a list of companies under a labour boycott.

Canadian Network for Ethical Investment
    Box 1615
    Victoria, B.C.
    V8W 2X7

Criteria for evaluating corporate behaviour, a regular newsletter, a networker list, and seminars on ethical investment.

Don Abrams and Time Buyer Associates
    P.O. Box 15891
    Station F
    Ottawa, Ont.
    K2C 3S8

Information on salary-deferral arrangements.

Ethicscan Canada
    P.O. Box 165
    Station S
    Toronto, Ont.
    M5M 4L7

A private company producing company profiles and other publications on corporate ethical performance in Canada.

Greenpeace Canada
    2623 West 4th Ave.
    Vancouver, B.C.
    V6K 1P8

Can provide advice to investors on the environmental record of companies and other prospective investments.

Project Ploughshares
    Conrad Grebel College
    Waterloo, Ont.
    N2L 3G6

Explores problems of disarmament and underdevelopment through research, publication, education and advocacy.

SACTU Solidarity Committee (Canada)
    P.O. Box 490
    Postal Station J
    Toronto, Ont.
    M4J 4Z2

SACTU is the South African Congress of Trade Unions; provides lists of Canadian companies with South African activities, including investment, imports and exports.

The Social Investment Forum
    711 Atlantic Ave.
    Boston, Mass
    02111

Presents socially responsible investment to the U.S. public, fosters the growth of the social-investment market and movement and facilitates

communication and cooperation among social-investment professionals.

Taskforce on the Churches and Corporate Responsibility
    129 St. Clair Ave. W.
    Toronto, Ont.
    M4V 1N5

Assists the major Christian churches in implementing policies in the
area of corporate social responsibility, issues a variety of publications
on corporate responsibility.

Alternative Investment Information

Canadian Jobs Strategy
    Place du Portage
    Phase IV, 4th Floor
    140 Promenade du Portage
    Hull, Quebec
    K1A 0J9

A program of the federal Department of Employment and Immigration. Can provide information on local Community Futures projects,
which may or may not solicit funds from individual investors.

Co-Operative Work (Toronto) Ltd.
    348 Danforth Ave.
    2nd Floor
    East Wing
    Toronto, Ont.
    M4K 1N8

Consulting group for cooperative and alternative business.

Development Incentives Inc.
    P.O. Box 1204
    Guelph, Ont.
    N1H 6N6

Consulting group for cooperative and alternative business.

Employment Co-operative Program
Co-operative Development Branch
8th Floor
215 Garry Street
Winnipeg, Man.
R3C 4J9

A Manitoba government program; provides financial and technical assistance to cooperatives.

National Association of Community Development Loan Funds
151 Montague City Road
Greenfield, Mass.
01301

Provides information on about thirty community funds in the United States.

Social Investment Study Group
c/o Ted Jackson
E.T. Jackson and Associates
Suite 712
151 Slater Street
Ottawa, Ont.
K1P 5H3

Conducts studies of ethical and alternative investment in Canada. E.T. Jackson and Associates also is a consulting group for cooperative and alternative business.

La Société de développement des coopératives
430 Chemin Sainte-Foy
Quebec City, Quebec.
G1S 2J5

A Quebec crown corporation providing financial and technical assistance to Quebec cooperatives and small business.

Westcoast Information and Research Cooperative
   10, 4965 Argyle St.
   Port Alberni, B.C.
   V9Y 1V6

Consulting group for cooperative and alternative businesses.

Working Margins Consulting Group
   200 — 651 Croydon Avenue
   Winnipeg, Man.
   R3M 0W3

Consulting group for cooperative and alternative businesses.

Worker Ownership Development Foundation
   348 Danforth Avenue
   2nd Floor, East Wing
   Toronto, Ont.
   M4K 1N8

Publishes information, sponsors conferences and meets with government representatives on worker cooperative issues.

Financial Information

Canadian Association of Financial Planners
   One First Canadian Place
   P.O. Box 24
   Suite 5900
   Toronto, Ont.
   M5X 1K2

Provides consumer information on financial planners.

Canadian Association of Investment Clubs
   c/o A.D.H. Smith
   Suite 3700
   First Canadian Place
   Toronto, Ont.
   M5X 1E9

Non-profit organization dedicated to teaching Canadians the proper way to invest through the medium of the investment clubs.

Investment Dealers Association of Canada
    Suite 350
    33 Yonge Street
    Toronto, Ont.
    M5E 1G4

Provides list of investment dealers.

Canadian Securities Institute
    Suite 360
    33 Yonge St.
    Toronto, Ont.
    M5E 1G4

Sponsors securities courses for investors and investment professionals and publishes booklets of interest to schools and the investing public.

Tax Issues

Elections Canada
    440 Coventry Road
    Ottawa, Ont.
    K1A 0M6

Provides list of registered political parties and other information on the political contributions tax credit.

Conscience Canada Inc.
    The Peace Tax Fund Committee
    505 — 620 View Street
    Victoria, B.C.
    V8W 2P3

Operates a trust account for taxpayers to deposit proportion of military-related taxes, sponsoring a Charter of Rights challenge on the right to withhold taxes for military purposes.

Publications

Don Abrams. *The Time Buyer*. Toronto: Deneau, 1986. Provides extensive information on salary-deferral arrangements.

Directory of Socially Responsible Investments (write c/o Funding Exchange, 666 Broadway, 5th Floor, New York, N.Y., 10012). A guide to ethical and alternative investment in the U.S.

Eva Innes, Robert L. Perry and Jim Lyon. *The Financial Post Selects the 100 Best Companies to Work for in Canada.* Toronto: Totem Books, 1987.

Constance Mungall. *More than Just a Job.* Ottawa: Steel Rail Publishing, 1986. Profiles a number of worker cooperatives in Canada.

Ernie Regehr. *Arms Canada: The Deadly Business of Military Exports.* Toronto: Lorimer, 1987. Provides a list of companies with military production, and other information about Canadian arms production.

Worker Co-ops (write c/o Center for the Study of Co-operatives, Diefenbaker Centre, University of Saskatchewan, Saskatoon, Sask., S7N 0W0). Covers all aspects of the worker cooperative movement in Canada.

APPENDIX 4

Canadian Ethical Mutual Funds Available to Individuals

All-Canadian Environmental Investment Fund/International Environmental Investment Fund

Sponsor:

Energy Probe of Toronto, Canada's leading energy and environmental advocacy group. The funds began as a private investment club of Energy Probe. In 1987, a sister-organization of Energy Probe received approval to offer the funds to the public in Ontario.

Manager:

E.I.F. Funds Management Ltd. of Toronto, a company owned and controlled by Energy Probe's treasurer to manage the Environmental Investment Funds.

Startup date:

September 15, 1987.

Ethical criteria:

The funds avoid investing in companies that have poor records with regard to the environment, military involvement and human rights.

Financial performance:

No data yet available.

Assets:

No data yet available.

RRSP/RRIF eligible:

All-Canadian fund — yes.
International fund — no.

Fees:

A one-time administrative fee of up to $100 will be charged for an initial purchase to open an Environmental Investments Fund account. No fees will be charged for subsequent purchases or withdrawals.

Minimum investment:

None.

Available from:

Available by writing to: Environmental Investment Funds Ltd.
    100 College Street
    6th Floor
    Toronto, Ont.
    M5G 1L5

Ethical Growth Fund

Sponsor:

Vancouver City Savings Credit Union. A community credit union, Van-City is the largest credit union in the country and the second-largest in the world.

Manager:

Connor, Clark and Lunn Investment Management Ltd. of Toronto. Connor, Clark and Lunn is a major pension-management company that provides services for pension-fund sponsors, corporations and individual investors.

Startup date:

February 3, 1986.

Ethical criteria (from the simplified prospectus):

"The fund will be socially responsible (meaning, the Fund will use specified ethical and moral standards in making investments) and the monies of the Fund will only be invested in securities of a Canadian corporation which meets the criteria established from time to time by the board of directors of the Trustee (sponsor). For these purposes, the following criteria must be met on any investment in a Canadian corporation.

1. The corporation must have either its registered or head office located in Canada and its shares must be either traded or about to be traded on a stock exchange in Canada.

2. The corporation should encourage progressive industrial relations with all members of its staff or employees. Initially in order to determine the corporations within this criterion, a review of current publications relating to employment practices is conducted and specific analysis is made of any corporations on any published 'hot lists.' From time to time thereafter published reports are followed (particularly at the time of any labour strife) to determine if there is any pattern of significant deterioration whereby a corporation would be considered for removal from the Fund's investment portfolio.

3. The corporation should regularly conduct business in, or with, a country or countries that provide racial equality within its or their political boundaries.

4. The normal business of the corporation should be the provision of products or services for civilians (non-military).

5. If the corporation is an energy corporation or utility, its major source of revenue should be from non-nuclear forms of energy."

Financial performance:

Rate of return was 7.41 per cent in the first six months and 15.1 per cent in the first year. In the first six months of 1987, the fund earned 8.97 per cent.

Assets:

$16.03 million (June 1987)

RRSP/RRIF eligible:

Yes

Fees:

Acquisition fees (front-end charges) of:

Amount invested	fee
up to $49,000	not more than 5%
$50,000 to $99,000	not more than 4%
$100,000 to $249,000	not more than 3%
$250,000 to $499,000	not more than 2%
$500,000 and over	not more than 1%

Minimum investment:

$500 for an initial purchase, $100 for subsequent purchases

Available from:

Generally available from mutual-fund brokers across the country and branches of Vancouver City Savings Credit Union in Vancouver.
For information, write: VanCity Investment Services Ltd.
Vancouver City Savings Credit Union
P.O. Box 24807
Postal Station C
Vancouver, B.C.
V5T 4E9

Investors Summa Fund Ltd.

Sponsor:

Investors Syndicate Ltd. of Winnipeg. A subsidiary of Investors Group Inc., a major provider of financial services to individuals and corporations. Investors Group is controlled by Power Financial Corp. of Montreal, a large holding company with interests in life insurance, trust and other financial companies.

Manager:

I.G. Investment Management Ltd. of Winnipeg, a subsidiary of Investors Group.

Startup date:

January 12, 1987.

Ethical criteria (from the simplified prospectus):

"The policy of the fund is directed towards investing in those companies which are socially responsive and have adopted progressive standards illustrative of an awareness towards economic, social and environmental issues. In particular, the Fund intends to refrain from investing in those companies whose primary activities, in the informed opinion of the Manager, include:

1) The manufacture and/or distribution of alcohol and tobacco products;

2) Gambling and projects related to gambling;

3) The manufacture of critical weapons systems;

4) The production, importation or distribution of pornographic material;

The Investment Manager will also make a concerted effort to exclude from the Fund's portfolio any companies:

1) which have failed to adopt and administer effective pollution control and environmental protection policies;

2) whose practices openly or passively support the acts of repressive régimes."

Financial performance:

Rate of return was 5.88 per cent at April 30, 1987.

Assets:

$25.87 million (April 30, 1987)

RRSP/RRIF eligible:

Yes.

Fees:

Amount of purchase	Sales charge as % of amount paid by the purchaser
To $24,999	8.5%
$25,000 to 49,999	8.0%
$50,000 to 74,999	7.0%
$75,000 to 99,999	6.0%

$100,000 to $149,999	5.0%
$150,000 to $199,999	4.0%
$200,000 to $299,999	3.0%
$300,000 and over	2.0%

Minimum investment:

$1,000 for an initial non-registered account. $500 for an initial RRSP/RRIF account. $50 for subsequent investments.

Available from:

Generally available from mutual-fund dealers across Canada and offices of Investors Syndicate Ltd. in major cities across Canada and Les Services Investors Limitée in Quebec. For information, write: Investors Summa Fund Ltd.

> 280 Broadway
> Winnipeg, Man.
> R3C 3B6

Le Fonds de solidarité des travailleurs du Québec (Quebec Federation of Labour Solidarity Fund)

Sponsor:

Quebec Federation of Labour. The fund was conceived by the Q.F.L. during the recession of 1981-82 as a way to channel the savings of Quebec working people into enterprises that will maintain and create new jobs in Quebec. One of the largest venture capital funds in the province, the fund invests money according to positive criteria and takes an active role in attempting to shape the Quebec economy.

It was set up under special Quebec legislation and has been granted special tax status by the Quebec and federal governments (see chapter 4 on taxation for a rundown of the tax savings). The fund is available for sale in Quebec only.

Manager:

The fund manages its own investments.

Startup date:

June 23, 1983.

Ethical criteria (from the information circular):

"Pursuant to the act, the Fund's principal objectives are:

a) to invest in Quebec enterprises and to provide its help to such enterprises for the purpose of creating, maintaining and safeguarding jobs;

b) to encourage the economic awareness and the training of workers and to increase their influence on the economic development of Quebec;

c) to stimulate the Quebec economy by means of strategic investments which will be for the benefit of workers in Quebec as well as Quebec business enterprises themselves;

d) to encourage the development of Quebec business enterprises by inviting labour to participate in such development by subscribing to shares of the Fund."

Financial performance:

Shares in the fund are valued twice a year. Rate of return for the year ending Oct. 31, 1985 was 5.1%. For the year ending April 30, 1986, 8.9%.

Assets:

$95 million (March, 1987)

RRSP/RRIF eligible:

RRSP — yes.

RRIF — no. Shares in the fund must be repurchased by the fund when a holder reaches the age of sixty, if he or she is retired or on early retirement, or by age sixty-five.

Fees:

There are no fees for share purchases. RRSP shareholders are charged an annual fee of $10 for an active plan and $4 for an inactive plan.

Minimum investment:

There are no minimum investments.

Available from:

Nearly 500 businesses in Quebec offer the fund to their employees through a weekly payroll-deduction plan. It is also available by writing to: Fonds de solidarité des travailleurs du Québec

      500 Sherbrooke St. W.
      Suite 1450
      Montreal, Que.
      H3A 3C6

APPENDIX 5

Portfolios of Three Canadian Ethical Mutual Funds[1]

Crown Commitment Fund (securities initially purchased when the fund started in September, 1986)

Gold
    International Corona Resources Ltd.
    Sherrgold Ltd.

Oil/ Gas
    Shell Canada Ltd.
    Total Petroleum Ltd.

Paper/Forest
    Consolidated Bathurst Ltd.

Consumer Products
    Hayes-Dana Inc.

Industrial Products
    CDC Life Sciences Inc.
    Haley Industries Ltd.
    Spar Aerospace Ltd.
    Moore Corp.

Merchandising
    Canadian Tire Ltd.
    Dylex Ltd.

[1]Since companies are added or dropped from time to time, these portfolios pertain only to the dates listed.

Real Estate
  Atlantic Shopping Centres Ltd.
  Campeau Corp.

Media
  Thomson Newspapers Ltd.
  Torstar Corp.

Financial Services
  Bank of Montreal
  National Bank of Canada

Management Companies
  Canadian Pacific Ltd.
  Jannock Ltd.

Ethical Growth Fund (June 30, 1987)

Gold
  Galactic Resources Ltd.

Oil/Gas
  Nova Corp.
  Canadian Roxy Petroleum Ltd.
  Canadian Occidental Petroleum Ltd.

Mining/Metals
  Breakwater Resources Ltd.

Paper/Forest
  British Columbia Forest Products Ltd.
  MacMillan Bloedel Ltd.
  Paperboard Industries Corp.

Consumer Products
  Budd Canada Inc.
  Core-Mark International Inc.

Industrial Products
  Canadian Satellite Communications Inc.
  Cinram Ltd.
  Great Pacific Industries Inc.
  Indal Ltd.
  Mitel Corp.

Xerox Canada Inc.

Transportation
Finning Ltd.

Financial Services
Bank of Montreal
Canadian Imperial Bank of Commerce
Great-West Life Co. Inc.
Lonvest Corp.
Royal Bank of Canada

Management Companies
Canadian Pacific Ltd.
Federal Industries Ltd.
Imasco Ltd.
International Pagurian Corp. Ltd.

Investors Summa Fund (February, 1987)

Consumer Products
Campbell Soup Ltd.
Canada Packers Inc.
Noma Inc.
Northern Telecom Ltd.

Industrial Products
Gandalf Technologies Inc.
IBM
Xerox Canada Inc.

Merchandising
Oshawa Group
Provigo Inc.

Real Estate
Cambridge Shopping Centres

Media
Maclean Hunter Ltd.
Moffat Communications
Torstar Corp.

Transportation
Laidlaw Transporation Ltd.

Utilities
B.C. Telephone
Maritime Telegraph and Telephone Co.

Financial Services
Bank of Montreal
Bank of Nova Scotia
Canadian Imperial Bank of Commerce
National Bank
Royal Bank
Toronto Dominion Bank
Trilon Financial Corp.

Management Companies
Bell Canada Enterprises

APPENDIX 6

U.S. Ethical Mutual Funds Available to Individuals

Calvert Social Investment Fund/Managed Growth Portfolio, Money Market Portfolio

Founded in 1982, the funds select investments in products and services that sustain the natural environment, are managed with employee participation, have fair negotiations with workers in an environment supportive of their well-being, have opportunities for women and minority groups, have an awareness of a commitment to goals such as creativity, productivity, self- respect, responsibility within the organization and the world, have no nuclear production, no South African business activity and no production of weapons systems. Minimum initial investment of $1,000 and minimum subsequent investments of $250. Fees range from 1% to 4.5%.
1700 Pennsylvania Avenue, N.W.
Washington, D.C.
20006

Dreyfus Third Century Fund

Launched in 1972, the fund is the largest of the American ethical investment funds. It evaluates investments on the basis of the contribution they make to four "areas of special concern": protection and improvement of the environment and proper use of natural resources, occupational health and safety, consumer protection and product purity and equal employment opportunity. The fund may also invest up to one- third of its total assets in companies that "contribute to the enhancement of the quality of life in America" by developing products, services, or technology related to the areas of concern or the fields of health, housing, education, or transportation. Minimum initial investment of $2,500 and minimum subsequent investments of $100. No sales charges if purchased directly from Dreyfus.

767 Fifth Avenue
New York, N.Y.
10153

New Alternatives Fund

Started in 1982, the philosophy of the fund is that investments made in petroleum resources will become increasingly less attractive than investments in non-petroleum resources. The fund invests in companies involved in solar and alternative energy initiatives, such as photovoltaic cells, energy conservation, architectural systems with solar heating, natural gas, biomass, hydro-electricity, wind turbines, geothermal systems and ocean wave energy production. Minimum initial investment of $2,650 and minimum subsequent investments of $500. Fees range from 3% to 6%.

295 Northern Boulevard
Great Neck, N.Y.
11021

Parnassus Fund

The fund started in 1984. From a financial viewpoint, Parnassus describes itself as a "contrarian" fund, which means that it purchases stock selling at a price that is depressed compared with the market as a whole and with its own history. From an ethical viewpoint, the fund invests in companies that fulfill five so-called "Renaissance factors": quality products and services, market-orientation and customer service, sensitivity to communities in which companies operate, employee treatment and innovation and response to change.

Minimum initial investment of $5,000 and minimum subsequent investments of $1,000. Fees range from 0.1% to 3.5%.

244 California Street
San Francisco, California
94111

Pax World Fund

Pax World, started in 1970, was the first ethical fund to be established
in the United States. It was founded by staff members of the United
Methodist Church Board of Social Concerns, who felt it was improper
to profit from the Vietnam War. It excludes investments in companies
that are engaged in military activities or liquor, tobacco and gambling
industries. It seeks out companies with fair-employment and pollution-
control practices. It also invests in some international development.
Minimum initial investment of $250 and minimum subsequent invest-
ments of $50. No front-end loads or redemption charges.

224 State Street
Portsmouth, New Hampshire
03801

The Pioneer Group

There is some controversy in the ethical investment movement about
whether the Pioneer Group should be classified as a group of ethical
funds. The group managers avoid South African, alcohol and tobacco
investments, but there are no ethical criteria included in the prospectuses issued for their funds. In addition, fund representatives say they
are not proponents of strategies such as "moral investing." Minimum
investments and fees vary with different funds in the group.

60 State Street
Boston, Massachusetts
02109

Working Assets Money Fund/Working Assets VISA Card

The Working Assets organization is a socially responsible financial organization, but it does not operate mutual funds like the other U.S. investment funds listed above. Instead, Working Assets operates a money
fund, which provides daily-interest chequing account services to investors. In addition, it offers a Visa card for people interested in having
an ethically minded credit-card service. The money fund avoids investments in weapons, nuclear power, South Africa, toxic waste- producing companies and companies that discriminate against minorities. It
seeks out organizations involved in housing, education, farming, small

business and energy conservation. When customers become holders of the Visa card, Working Assets contributes $2 to non-profit organizations working for peace, human rights, a clean environment and aid to the hungry. With each card transaction, Working Assets contributes five cents to these organizations.

> 230 California Street
> San Francisco, California
> 94111

APPENDIX 7

Canadian Ethical Mutual Funds Available to Pension Plans, Charitable Organizations, Group RRSPs and Other Institutions

Canadian Alternative Investment Co-operative (CAIC)

CAIC was founded in 1984 by ten Canadian religious institutions and continues to be dominated by religious organizations such as the Jesuit Centre for Social Faith and Justice in Toronto, a religious newspaper and a number of Catholic dioceses. However, membership in CAIC is open to any organization registered as a charity under the Income Tax Act. CAIC aims to invest 60 per cent of its funds in mortgages for urban renewal programs, cooperative housing and other social housing. About 20 per cent of the fund is slated for social mortgages, such as group homes for religious communities, which will pay a lower rate of interest. Ten per cent of the fund is slated to be approved for community economic development projects and 10 per cent is to go toward venture-capital loans on high- risk projects undertaken by cooperatives and non-profit organizations.

> P.O. Box 160
> Station V
> Toronto, Ont.
> M6R 3A5

Canadian Ethical Dynamic And Responsible (CEDAR) Balanced Fund

Established in 1986, CEDAR is open to Canadian pension funds as well as other non-taxable organizations, such as foundations, unions and religious organizations. The fund is managed by C.E.D.A.R. Investment Services Ltd. The principals in C.E.D.A.R. Investment are Crawford Laing of Vancouver, a consulting actuary, and Roger Laing of Edmonton, a former social worker.

CEDAR screens investments according to eight criteria: international (business in countries whose governments are oppressive), military, nuclear (development, production and sale of nuclear energy), environment (environmentally unsound practices in resource extraction, waste, protection of the ecosystem and endangered species), community relations, ethical standards, employee relations (disregard for equality, dignity, health and safety of workers) and consumer products (harmful products). Preference is given to corporations that develop and use renewable energy sources, follow responsible environmental practices, are sensitive to their communities and employees and employ superior product design.

> #1, 10005 — 80 Avenue
> Edmonton, Alta.
> T6E 1T4

Crown Commitment Fund

Crown Commitment Fund was established in 1986 by Crown Life Insurance Co. of Toronto as an ethical fund for pension plans and group RRSPs. Investments are screened for corporate citizenship (community contributions, codes of ethics, record of philanthropy, product quality and safety, truthful advertising), employee relations (industry leader in employee relations, good-faith bargaining, no history of lockouts or strikebreaking, good health and safety record, no discrimination by age, sex or race, wages competitive with industry averages), weapons manufacturing, South African trade (no current business, and a policy not to enter or return to South Africa), environmental sensitivity (not harmful, working to minimize environmental impact and strong concern for the environment). Companies classified as marginal in terms of these criteria may be considered for investment if they are clearly seen to be moving to meet the criteria.

> Crown Life Insurance Co.
> 120 Bloor Street East
> Toronto, Ont.
> M4W 1B8